John
of
God

Journey to the Spirit World

John
of
God

Journey to the Spirit World

Kelsie McKinney
MPS, LPC, LMHC

Roots and Wings Publishing

Address all inquiries to:
Roots and Wings Publishing
1750 30th Street, #631
Boulder, CO 80301

First edition – First printing
Printed in the United States

ISBN 0-9777493-0-4
    978-0-9777493-2-4

A heartfelt thanks goes to Kay Turnbaugh for the cover design and interior design of this book.

Cover image © Somesun | Dreamstime.com

Dedication

*To Medium Joao
who has selflessly devoted his life
to healing the sick
and easing human suffering*

Thank you

CONTENTS

87 △ chapter 6

Home Again, Home Again

My ankle heals... my back adjusts...

healing's happening everywhere!

Dr. Wayne Dyer and his leukemia healing

97 △ chapter 7

New Friends, Old Friends, and the Dogs of the Casa

A new reality

I want my miracle NOW!

Ruthann's story

The dogs of the Casa

Sitting in current, and sitting in current,

and sitting in current!

119 △ chapter 8

Sharing These Blessings with Others

chapter 1

Why Would a Smart Girl Like You Go to the Middle of Brazil for Healing?!

As I sit in Abadiania, Brazil, I begin to write my story with great resistance. But, the Entities – the good spirits that come through John of God – insist this story be told. As you read on you will understand why I have a hard time writing my personal story. My mind tells me that negative consequences are possible. Yet, these Entities are insisting that I tell this story and what brought me to this most amazing man called John of God. It has been a deep and profound journey – a journey to the spirit world.

My story begins almost seven years ago while living in the mountains of Colorado. I had just finished writing my first book, *Migraines Be Gone.* As the book was coming to completion, I longed for more connection to people again. Writing a book is a very solitary experience and I tend to be a social person. One night while sitting in one of the most magnificent hot springs in Colorado, I awaited the full moon rise over the San Juan Mountains. There were several of us in the springs watching the glow from behind the mountain range and we sat in awe waiting for what was to be a very large full moon. It was a magical night indeed.

After the moon came up our silence gradually broke as we all came out of a trance like state. I began talking to the man next to me whom I shall call Richard. For the next three and a half months Richard and I spent most of our weekends together... hiking in the beautiful Rocky Mountains, watching sunsets, cooking wonderful meals together, sitting in front of my fireplace, and having conversations that went long into the night. It was an amazing time for both of us as we played and got to know each other. Richard appeared to be the perfect man... charming, highly intelligent, well-dressed, caring, compassionate, romantic, very good looking, and he had a great sense of humor.

Things are not as they appear

In May we were heading to New York State for my mother's 80th birthday. In the days before we were to leave I could sense some agitation in Richard and he started saying things that shocked me and rattled me to the core. The first one I remember was that he suggested we take life insurance policies out on each other. Stunned, I thought "What a bizarre thing to say to someone that you have been dating for less than four months!" But, I was very focused on preparing for the trip and for my first public talk/ book signing in New York so I just let it go.

A few days later Richard told me that his second wife died two weeks after he found out that she had opened a separate checking account. He added that it was easier to have her die than to be left, saying that he could not handle a woman leaving him. Losing a woman to death was his preference, he said. I felt my blood run cold. Richard had two dead wives. The first one died shortly after she left him and the second one died as she had planned to leave.

What occurred over the next three years is almost hard to believe. I am leaving the details out of this story as I do not want this to be a book of terror. My intention is that this book will be one of hope, second chances, love, and life as I share just enough with you so that you understand how much healing I needed in my life.

While in New York I was kidnapped by Richard, taken to a deserted wooded area, and told that I would never see my family again. Though I did not think I would live through the night, obviously, it was not my time to go. This was a man who had enough control to stay out of jail and anything he was to do would be very calculated and planned out. And that is what saved me as several people knew we were together and there would be no way out for him.

At one point he put a knife to my throat and said, "There is nothing like a good clean kill." That expression, I later learned, means that someone kills and gets away with it and then goes on with their life as though nothing had happened... a good, clean kill. As my blood again ran cold the spirits spoke to me... as they have on occasion since my childhood. They told me very clearly that neither one of his wives died "accidentally." They had, in fact, died at his hands according to what I was hearing from spirit communication. It was not clear if there were others but what became clear over time was that this was a game for him... hunting, stalking, striking, and terrorizing women.

When the kidnapping episode was over it was clear that I would never be able to return to my home in the mountains where I lived alone. I have very fond memories of my home... many friends visited... we watched sunsets, had great parties, good conversation, meditation, nature, and lots of laughter. Indeed, my home had been filled with beautiful, fun and loving energy. It all ended that night and I was never able to spend another night in my home again.

This was the beginning of my entire life crumbling into millions of small pieces. As I could not return home to live, and I did not know where I was going, I was forced to leave my beloved cat, Tula, behind. This broke my heart in a very deep way as any kitty lover can imagine. She was the most magnificent cat and we had a very deep bond. Some loving Buddhists took her into their community to be nurtured and cared for. They knew how special she was and they were totally thrilled to take her. I was comforted in knowing that she went to a good home yet when I returned some time later to pick up my personal belongings my heart sank. All her things were gone... her kitty bed, her kitty dish, and all her kitty toys... and there was a hole in my heart. This was the beginning of everything in my life being ripped away from me.

My life as I knew it gets ripped away

I disappeared without a trace from this little mountain town and did not even say a good-bye. There were to be no good-byes to friends as intense stalking had already begun and it was critical that no one knew where I was. To leave my home town and people I had connected with, without even saying good-bye, was also heart wrenching. But, now I was on the run from someone who was threatening to find me and murder me in the most violent way. And, I knew he was both serious with his threats and capable of it. I also knew that he would only do it in a very calculated way in which he would not get caught.

Initially the threats came through emails and messages left in my voice mail that sent my blood running cold. There would be up to twenty five email messages a day and it was clear that there was some obsessive thinking going on inside this man. Chilling messages left in my voice mail box continued daily until I finally surrendered to leaving the box full so that no more messages could be left. It became clear that I needed to get a restraining order to stop the violent communications and intrusion... at least I thought it would stop this craziness.

I had always been a person who talked quite openly about my life. Initially, I began talking to people about what was going on and I was shocked to hear so many stories of women who had been stalked, abused, and murdered. People told me stories of their sisters, their friends, and their daughters... some who managed to get out and some who were trapped for various reasons. Suddenly, I was seeing a whole side of life I had not been exposed to before.

It was interesting to me that I had never heard any stories like this before… except on television. It was something that happened to someone else, I thought. For sure, I was immune to this. I thought it ran in families! Eventually, I, too, stopped talking about it as I discovered first hand the intense discrimination towards women who are abused by men.

Society's sting

My first sting of harsh judgment came from a man I had known for about ten years. As I struggled to figure out how to deal with this whole situation, I knew the first thing I needed to do was find a safe place to live. In the most raw and vulnerable place of my life, I reached out to this friend and told him the story. He is a Licensed Counselor and I was sure that I would feel compassion and understanding from him… and maybe even find a temporary place to stay while I figured out my next step. Instead I received a curt response as he said only, "You should have seen it coming."

This kind of judgment was common and was like a knife through my heart. It added pain to the open wound which was already bleeding profusely, but, I still continued talking to people and reaching out for help. Next, I went to Boulder's most popular church which I had attended for some years. Surely I would receive some support and compassion here. After all, this is what the minister preached. His words of wisdom to me were "Think positive thoughts and all will be good." Again, I had hoped for some compassion and maybe help finding a temporary place to stay! But, these were the words I got before being sent out the door. I thought, "Will positive thinking stop the stalking and death threats?!" I was beginning to feel very alone and that no one understood.

At this point I was talking openly about the situation at the meditation center I had been connected with for twenty seven years. One of the center leaders told me to not talk about this part of my life. Then he added, "You created this whole thing because you like it on some level." His psychoanalysis of me was both painful and completely inaccurate. Granting him his wish, I kept the details of my life held within thereafter.

So, early on I was silenced by the two "spiritual" centers in Boulder I had been connected with. The message was, "If you don't think about it or talk about it, then it doesn't exist. Just think happy thoughts!" Okay… I do love Boulder but does this mean that if we don't talk about violence against women it won't exist? Is it possible to talk about difficulties in life and still be considered on a spiritual path!? Is there no room for compassion? Many questions were coming up for me…

I wandered aimlessly not knowing how to handle my new life situation. Everything in my life was being stripped away... my home, my beloved cat, my sense of feeling safe in the world, my sense of peace and even my ability to focus on my work as all of my energy was now going into keeping myself alive. For the first time in my life I was in "survival" mode... a place I had not been in before.

Soon enough I learned that technology is a stalkers dream come true. I asked many questions to the police and to the Women's Shelter about technologies and stalking and how to handle technology in this situation. No one knew the answers to my questions. I had to dig and dig to find the answers out myself. Meanwhile Richard continued to send messages in a variety of ways to let me know that he was hunting me – to use his words – and that he would keep on until he finds me. Then he promised a brutal and violent death.

Compassion where I least expected to find it

The permanent restraining order turned out to be only a "piece of paper," as they say. The sheriff in my county told me that I needed to get a gun and learn how to use it. He issued a concealed weapons permit and connected me with a retired army sergeant in Colorado Springs. Off I went to become a pistol packing mama! Now here is an interesting thing... the caring hearts I had been searching for... I found one in this Army sergeant. Apparently, he had worked with many women in similar situations and one of his daughters had been a victim of domestic violence. He trained me like an army sergeant would train... and he did it with compassion in his heart.

I began to find caring souls in the most unlikely places! Isn't life just funny sometimes!? Just as people have pre-conceived ideas about women who are abused by men, I certainly had preconceived ideas about people in the military. It is not where I would have expected to have found such a compassionate and caring heart.

Richard's communications to me continued on as he found ways to get around the restraining order without getting caught. His gruesome threats came in a variety of ways which need not be detailed here. As I was being stalked I was forced to always be alert and there was no room for relaxation. Wherever I was I found that I was constantly watching all that was around me. Feeling safe in the world was completely gone for me.

Eventually, I settled into a new living situation with a huge sigh of relief. Though the death threats continued I felt like I was in a place that was as safe as I could do. It would be very difficult to find me. By this time I was six months into the ordeal and was not exhausted by it all yet, but, with each punch I took...

both by this man and society... I felt my life force slipping away.

The challenge of being invisible

My plan with the release of my book was to do book signings and presentations and to become very visible with my work. That all changed as I was forced to stay small and hidden... out of the public eye and off of the Internet... doing business with a phone number which could not be in my name or published. What to do? I have always enjoyed teaching so I decided to offer some classes. Though this was not my plan, it was what life was now presenting me. So, I arranged to teach some classes through an adult education program but when I asked them to not put the location of my classes on the Internet I was told, "It sounds like you are endangering our students."

I was starting to experience discrimination with work due to the stalking. What could possibly go wrong next?! One very cold winter night I received a call from my landlady. She told me not to go back to the place I had rented as she had changed the locks on the door and I was no longer welcome there. I had, unfortunately, shared with her the fact that I was being stalked. She confiscated all of my personal and business belongings and all of my financial records. When the police came they recommended that I go elsewhere for the night as the landlady had a large threatening guy there to keep me out and the police were afraid that I would get hurt.

How could this be?! It is against the law in Boulder County to lock a tenant out…. even if they had not paid their rent… but, of course, I had paid rent. How could someone just throw me out on a five degree night in wintertime and get away with it? Ah, but they could because I was the one viewed as society's outcast… an abused woman… there must really be something wrong with me and therefore it was just fine to throw me out on the street.

In total disbelief of what was happening I went to a friend's house where I slept on her living room floor for several weeks. Feeling totally homeless, I was just starting to understand why abused women keep their mouths shut and hold it all in. At this point I had lost my home in the mountains, my beloved cat, and my freedom. I am beginning to experience discrimination in both housing and work. Now I am sleeping on a floor and someone has possession of all my belongings and financial records. Could things possibly get lower than this?

These kinds of complications from the stalking began to wear me down after time… even more than the death threats. In fact, there were times that I wished it would just all be over and death was what I hoped for more than once. The black hole kept getting bigger and deeper and this seemed the only way out. One time the authorities called me and told me that Richard was threatening to come to Boulder to murder me. By law, they had to let me know this and, as a Licensed Counselor, I understand this law. I also know the intelligent and cunning mind Richard has and I know that this was probably his way of communicating to me through using the system. The stalking was at the one year point when this happened and I was starting to wear. With every new message that would come to me from this man, or the authorities that were overseeing him, I felt re-traumatized. I was beginning to experience anxiety, depression and insomnia.

Whose movie am I in?!

I felt like I was in someone else's movie. I could not even begin to imagine how this could happen in my life. Life had been so good to me... I had a good education, always lived in very nice places, had been happy and content, had travel, friends, money came easily to me... laughter came easily, I meditated and ate good food, was healthy. This was unbelievable... and, yet, it was happening.

The first time the restraining order was broken was when I learned that the law was on his side... not on mine. Since then I have learned that many abusers will get the law on their side so they are protected. I remember calling the Sheriff in Richard's county to inform him that the restraining order had broken and that I had proof of it. The Sheriff responded with, "Hee, hee, hee... did Richard break a restraining order again?! Boys will be boys! Are you the one from Albuquerque?" "No," I said. "Another one!" he declared. "You're the fourth one now who has a restraining order on him... hee, hee, hee. Well, I'll have to swing by his house and remind him that he shouldn't break it... hee, hee, hee..." The sheriff treated it as one big joke. I began to feel more and more alone and helpless.

As I struggled to keep my head above water the stalking entered into a second year. Though my energy was fading I was encouraged to take a course in street fighting. This training was amazing and was very empowering to me. It is the kind of thing I never would have done had this situation not occurred. Again, I found deep compassion in the trainers... another place where I would not have expected to find such caring hearts. They, too, were familiar with domestic violence and had trained women before who were in my situation.

I would start to feel in my power... and, wham... I would be hit again with what felt like punches from both Richard and society. It was a roller coaster ride that seemed endless. Was there any way out? Would this ever end? Would I ever feel normal again? Would I ever laugh and feel joy again? These are the questions that went through my head as I wondered if I had been permanently damaged. To be traumatized by the initial kidnapping was one thing… it was over in a matter of hours. But, the stalking… the repeated trauma… was sucking the life out of my soul.

I eventually found a good therapist who understood stalking on all levels… the devastation it was taking on me emotionally, financially, and on my very soul. Therapy was expensive and I was forced to put all these therapy visits on credit cards while Richard received free counseling and group therapy from the state. No one paid for my therapy. It all seemed so unfair to me. When I submitted my counseling bills to his county they responded with, "You didn't end up in the hospital. You don't get counseling!"

Meanwhile, fighting for my life was costing a whole lot more than just therapy bills. When someone has cancer they just do what they need to do and deal with the finances later. It was the same for me. My home sat empty for a long time as I continued to pay bills on it while I scrambled to find a new place to live, stay safe, and create a new life.

The need to be silent

In the second year of stalking I just needed to stop talking to friends and family about what was going on. In her eighties now, my mom didn't need to hear the stories and I told her that everything was fine. Yet, somehow she knew and occasionally would have nightmares that he had found me and that she got a call from the hospital. The next morning she would call me and she was so grateful to learn that I was still alive.

My therapist knew more about my situation than anyone else. He was a very compassionate man and was encouraging me to move out of Colorado and to cut my long, curly red locks and to go with short, blond hair. Knowing all the details of this story, which I am omitting here, he even suggested changing my name. Then he removed any connection to his location from the web in the event I was kidnapped. Not only was he concerned about my safety but, now, he was concerned for his, as well. Yet, being drained at this point in time, I could not even consider the energy this would take.

As I entered into my third year of being stalked my mind wondered how someone could stalk a woman for so long... a woman he had dated for less than four months. I was now sinking into a hole of financial devastation on top of everything else. Still owning my home in the mountains, the housing market had plummeted leaving me with the expenses of a house I may never be able to live in again.

My friends who had supported me through the beginnings of this ordeal were still by my side but I did not talk about what was really going on in my life. Simply put, I needed to have some escape... to go to the movies with them... or a party... to dance and laugh a little again. What is the point in life if I cannot feel some joy? I became proficient at holding things in and this was very new for me. First, the holding in came out of the harsh judgment towards me... then the discrimination in work and housing... and, finally, of my own accord as I simply needed to escape from this horrible reality.

I cried a lot when I was alone and so many tears flowed that at times I wondered if it would ever stop. Life just did not make sense anymore. Unable to be visible in the world and do the work I wanted to do with public speaking, I felt my purpose was being stripped away. What can I give if I have to be invisible? How can I generate money to take care of myself if I have to be invisible? How is it possible that this could occur in my life?

A friend spoke highly of a man in southern New Mexico who claimed that he could interfere with the energetics and cause the stalking to stop. In desperation I flew down and spent some time with him spending a chunk of money I did not have and continuing to go deeper into the financial black hole. Though the time with him helped me to feel more in my power, the stalking soon started up and my personal power was ripped away once again. I felt violated, overwhelmed, and helpless. Someone had stolen my life... I was no longer in control of it.

During the three years that I was stalked several men came forward with connections to people who could just take care of this once and for all. They could see the pain I was in and knowing that the law was not doing anything to help me they felt I should just take matters into my own hands. I could not believe that my life had gone so low yet I opted to say no to their offers.

The dark night of my soul

Hopeless and helpless, my very soul felt dense and heavy... grey was the color. Someone else had control of my life and my energy was being drained from me. I was becoming depleted. Somehow I maintained my will to live but I would often think, "What is the point if there is no joy?" Somewhere deep inside of me there must have been some hope that joy and purpose would return to my life.

All that I had imagined doing had been stolen away from me... all my dreams were gone. My enthusiasm and excitement about my work had been ripped away. I felt broken and I did not know if I would ever recover. My life force was being sucked like a vampire would suck blood. It was a game of cat and mouse... and the mouse was getting weary.

In spite of my internal life being in shambles, I put on my happy face for Boulder. This is what was required, it seemed. When I went to my meditation center – the one where I was asked not to talk about this – I would smile and say I was doing great. People would say, "Things must be good for you. You're looking wonderful!" I would leave it at that and no longer could I participate in any of the social events because it was simply too hard to hold up this facade. Underneath a very thin veneer was a life that was completely ravaged, and, I would wonder how people could not see that. Maybe they just did not want to see it. It was not a pretty story. For the first time in my life I experienced a split between what was true for me and what I projected to the world. It was painful to not be able to honestly express what was happening in my life and I longed to be embraced regardless of what the circumstances in my life were. I felt completely fractured.

During the three years of stalking I ended up moving six times due to many bizarre circumstances. One time I found a little place I liked and signed a lease. When the landlord found out that the utilities were in a friend's name the landlord went ballistic and said I could not do that. He said it was against his lease and against the law. I was forced to tell him about the stalking and why the utilities were not in my name. He told me he didn't care and that he was sending me my security deposit back. These moves were taking a huge toll on me. I had no grounding and I felt completely homeless.

At one point I knew I needed to stand up for myself and get back into my power again. I decided to take the landlord who threw me out on the street to small claims court to recoup the costs from that ordeal. In Boulder County it is, supposedly, against the law to do a "lock-out" on your tenant.

Unbelievably, the judge twisted things around to say that I had moved out of my own accord. He said it was my decision! I was in total shock and never expected this. For sure the courts would be on my side, I thought. I had been locked out! I had no key to get in! How could he even say that I made the decision to move out!? But, he cut me off and wouldn't let me talk. I began to feel like I was society's outcast as an abused woman and, therefore, it was just fine to treat me this way and to rule however he wanted. It is legal, I learned, to discriminate against women who are being abused.

Somehow I got my strength up to appeal this decision and take it up one level in the judicial system. The law school at CU Boulder became my home for a few days as I researched other cases and made my case. I did a very thorough job and even had an attorney look it over. My attorney told me that the judge that ruled against me is known for doing whatever he wants with no regard for the law. He also told me that I should win this case but he added that the judge who had heard my case is friends with the judges at the district level and that they cover each other. They will not rule against one another.

This case certainly was not about money. It was about reclaiming my power again and asserting my rights. It was about wanting to believe that I was not alone and that someone was on my side. Yet, I received a totally devastating blow when it turned out that my attorney was right and the judges do cover one another's back.

This was probably the lowest point for me in the whole journey. I felt like society's outcast. There was no other reason for the judge to rule against me except that he viewed me as a low life that did not deserve justice. Having a cold blade of a knife against my throat was nothing compared to this. Truly I was in the dark night of the soul. I had yet another horrible blow to deal with. Feeling empty and alone, I had lost faith in life, justice, and in the goodness of humanity. There was deep sadness in my soul.

For twenty five years I had been a spiritual seeker. I had the great privilege of studying with the wisest spiritual teachers in the world, meditating whenever I wanted, traveling to India multiple times, living in ashrams and taking powerful therapy groups. I was constantly in the search of truth and doing all that is humanly possible to make sense of life and existence. Until I met Richard I lived in joy, peace and wonderment. Now, at the lowest point in my life, there was no joy or happiness. It was bleak and it did not make sense to me.

Light at the end of the tunnel

As I made new friends during this time I told them nothing of this story. After experiencing so much harsh judgment from people towards me for "creating this situation" in my life, I felt it was best to be silent. One of the new friends I made was Marianne Shell, a medical doctor. I had great respect for her and trusted her integrity and experience.

Marianne told me about her experiences with John of God in Brazil. I recalled seeing a documentary about him on television many years ago. When I saw the show I immediately dismissed it in my mind as "smoke and mirrors" and thought it was a "bunch of bull." But, now, hearing it from Marianne, I was listening. She described in detail the healing of her knee and her eye. I was fascinated to hear these stories from a medical doctor.

Then I happened to be talking to Dhanyam, another person I fully respected. Dhanyam lives in the San Francisco Bay Area and I originally met him in India many years ago. We were talking on the phone and he told me that in the late '90s he was diagnosed with incurable leukemia. The doctors had no treatment for the type of leukemia he had, so he made three trips to John of God over the course of three years, and gradually his blood counts improved. Now, almost fifteen years later he is healthy and well, with normal blood counts.

Next I met a woman, Cheryl, in Denver who told me she had been healed of breast cancer by John of God. She was scheduled for a mastectomy. Two days before her surgery she received a call from the doctor's office saying they needed to reschedule her and they booked her out an additional ten days.

Having gotten herself psychologically prepared for the surgery, it was difficult to have it postponed. Cheryl had heard of John of God and decided to go there and spend some time meditating, assuring her dad, a medical doctor, that she was just going to clear her head and that she would be back for the surgery. Long story short, she was healed of breast cancer and never had the surgery or any Western treatment. Today, many years later, she is still healthy and doing fine.

Suddenly people who had been healed by the spirits that come through John of God started appearing in my life. Perhaps when one is facing a crisis he/she becomes more open to experiencing divine healing. I had always thought I was open minded but when I saw that television show I was absolutely certain that this was not for real! Now, I began to wonder if this well-known healer could help me out with my life threatening situation…

chapter 2

Who is John of God?

An extra-ordinary life

Joao Teixeira de Faria (John of God) was born in 1942 to a poor family in the state of Goias in central Brazil. Joao was born with an amazing gift. What he has is not something that can be taught or transferred from person to person. His clairvoyant and psychic abilities became apparent when he was only a child.

One time when Joao was only nine he predicted that a horrible storm was coming into town which would destroy many houses. Though it was a calm and clear day, his mother listened to him and they moved out of harm's way. Soon a storm appeared from out of nowhere that damaged and destroyed about forty houses in this very small town.

As a young man he was forced to go to wherever he could to find work. One time when he was unemployed and far from home, he was lonely, tired, and hungry. He sought shelter under a bridge and he planned to bathe and refresh in the river. Then the spirit of a beautiful, young woman appeared to him. The woman, St. Rita de Cascia, told him to go to the Spiritist Center of Christ the Redeemer.

When he arrived at the center they were expecting him and at that moment Joao lost consciousness for some hours. When he became conscious he apologized to the crowd of people around him explaining that he had fainted from hunger. Someone then told him that the spirit of King Solomon had come through him and about fifty people had been healed. While at this Spiritist Center it became very clear to Joao that he was to devote his life to healing the sick and easing human suffering. His mission was to serve God and humanity.

Though he was loved by many, he was persecuted, beaten and jailed by others for his unconventional approach towards healing. Yet, he continued with his calling. At one point the persecutions became so bad that the Brazilian military took him in. He did healings for the military personnel and their families for nine years in exchange for protection. Eventually the Entities –

the saints, doctors, and other good spirits that come through him – insisted that he could no longer limit himself to a privileged few. The Entities agreed that they would take care of him if he would devote himself to humanity.

Joao spent many years traveling to help people wherever he could. This was, of course, very wearing on him. Then, after years of traveling, a message came through a very well known and loved Brazilian medium (a person who can communicate with spirits) named Francisco "Chico" Xavier. Chico Xavier was a friend and mentor to Joao. The message that came through instructed Joao to establish a sanctuary in Abadiania, a small village in central Brazil, where people could come to him for healing. The Casa de Dom Inacio de Loyola was established. It is often referred to simply as the Casa, meaning "house." It is a house of love and healing.

Joao worked very hard at the Casa and continued to travel to help people who could not afford to come to Abadiania. As his fame grew the number of sick showing up multiplied. While working many years ago he began to feel quite sick and Joao, who had been burning the candle at both ends, suffered a massive stroke.

Joao was taken to the hospital to see where the brain blockage had occurred. Just as the test began all of the equipment failed! Repairs were quickly carried out and the tests resumed. Once again the equipment mysteriously burned out. The doctors prepared Joao for surgery but when they weren't looking he slipped out of the hospital and returned back to the Casa as he wanted to continue on with his mission. He was only 45 years old and the stroke left him paralyzed down one side of his body.

In spite of his paralysis he carried on with his healing work. He continued in this way for some months and eventually the Entities instructed Joao to operate on himself. Joao was guided to do an actual physical operation where he would cut into his body. Most of the operations that are performed are invisible and are on the soul level. The physical body does not get touched in an invisible surgery. In front of a fascinated crowd, he performed a visible surgery cutting into his chest with no signs of discomfort. To everyones delight, he was renewed and his paralysis was gone.

After surviving many years of persecution, Joao Teixeira de Faria later received many high honors for his work. Though several court cases have been brought against him, they have been dismissed as a result of his healing many high officials and their families. They can no longer say he is a fraud and they seem to protect him now and keep him out of jail so that he can proceed with his work.

John of God ("Joao de Deus" in Portuguese) is a medium. A medium is a person who communicates with spirits. There are many different types of mediums and many ways that spirits can communicate to the living. Sometimes mediums will hear a voice from a spirit and will pass the message on. There are popular television shows with mediums that do this and they communicate messages from loved ones. A medium may see images and receive their communication from the spirit world visually. Other times the spirit will take over the voice of the medium and the message will come through as they speak. Some mediums allow the spirit to control their body and automatic writing is what comes through.

John of God, or Medium Joao, is a full trance medium. This means that he is not conscious during the healings and he will not remember anything of what has happened during that time. He is in a full trance while he allows the Entities to use his body to do the healing work. Spirits of saints and great doctors who have already passed into the spirit world come through John of God and use his body to heal people. This type of mediumship is rare and is a great gift to the world.

The spirits that come through are referred to as Entities. There are about thirty seven that come through on a regular basis and reportedly thousands of other good spirits, called a "phalange" of spirits, are hovering around assisting with the work. All of these Entities hope to help alleviate human pain and suffering. It is a part of their evolution to be here helping.

Catholicism and Spiritism

Brazil is predominately a Catholic country and Joao himself was raised Catholic. He is also a Spiritist which is common in Brazil. At the Casa de Dom Inacio de Loyola where he does his work there is a feeling of both Catholicism and Spiritism in the air.

Spiritism is a body of faiths that has in common the belief of spirit after death. In a stricter sense, it is a philosophy based on the works of Allan Kardec and others. Allan Kardec is considered to be the father of Spiritism and he is best known for his classic book, *The Spirits' Book* (1856). This book is, by far, one of the most popular books about mediumship, spirits, and the evolution of the soul. Allan Kardec was French and Spiritism formed in France in the 19th century. Today it is found throughout the world but primarily in Brazil.

While some Spiritists see themselves as not adhering to a religion, but to a philosophical doctrine with a scientific basis, many Spiritists do not have a problem embracing it as a religion. In either case, what Spiritists have in common is a belief in the existence of spirits living in the invisible world and the possibility of communication between these spirits and living people.

Spiritism claims to be based on the teachings of Jesus Christ and their doctrine stresses the importance of spiritual evolution. Spiritists believe that each spirit faces many problems, obstacles, and situations that they need to learn to deal with in order to perfect themselves. According to their view, humanity is destined for perfection. I recommend the book *Introduction to the Spiritist Philosophy* by Allan Kardec if you would like to learn more about Spiritism.

Miracles and science

As a biofeedback therapist I have long been interested in bridging the gap between science and consciousness. I measure bodily functions that even fifty years ago doctors said we could not control. Medical biofeedback therapists measure such things as blood pressure, circulation, sweat gland activity, respiration, brain wave activity and muscle tension. We then teach our patients how to take conscious control of these functions in their bodies to eliminate their symptoms. We know they can do it because we get readings on the computer screen that show us the changes they are making in their body. Biofeedback is short for "biological feedback." Before the science of biofeedback doctors said these functions were involuntary and patients had no control over them. It is a beautiful dance between science and consciousness when working to help people to heal their symptoms using biofeedback.

Though yogis have known for centuries that we have control over these bodily functions, in our scientifically based culture it took biofeedback to convince people that they had this control. Likewise, Spiritists claim that there is a science behind the healings that come through Medium Joao and that there is a natural order to events in the universe. While the science of Spiritism will likely be slower to prove than what biofeedback came to prove, there are people who are actively working on developing the science behind this kind of healing.

For those of you who are scientists like myself, you might want to investigate the U.S. Spiritist Medical Congress. The U.S. Spiritist Medical Congress holds conferences which are not exclusive to healthcare professionals. The conferences are open to all those interested in learning about the mechanisms of spiritual healing and the effects of spirituality on human health. Spiritists will say that the healings that happen by the Entities that come through Medium Joao are not miracles. The science behind these healings has not been fully proven yet but there are people working to develop the understanding of how this occurs and how we can re-create such healings.

A miracle is often defined as "a surprising and welcome event that is not explicable by natural or scientific laws and is therefore considered to be the work of a divine agency." I do agree with Spiritists that there is a natural order to events. Since the science is not fully developed I will continue to use the word miracle. I say, "YES to miracles!" and, personally, I do not need the science behind the work of the Entities to know it is real. In fact, to me, it is even more special to experience these healings in the mystery of not knowing the science behind it.

Obsession and disobsession

Obsession, also known as spirit obsession, is generally believed by Spiritists to be a major factor in causing physical, mental, or emotional disorders. In fact, it is believed to be one of the most frequent causes of mental illness and criminal behavior. While people often think of obsession as being the influence of a spirit on a living being, it can take several other forms. This includes: a living person influencing another living being, a living person influencing a spirit, or a spirit influencing another spirit.

In the case of a spirit influencing a living being, the victim suffers but does not know where his suffering is coming from. The obsessed person may be led to behave abnormally without apparent reason and will not be able to explain his deeds or crimes. In the case of a living person obsessing another living person the victim usually knows where the influence is coming from but often does not know what to do about it. Another type of obsession occurs when the spirit of a deceased person is not able to break his bonds with the living, in which case both suffer.

Many things can motivate obsessors to do what they do. Envy, revenge, prejudice and sadism are often motivators for obsessors. If it is a spirit doing the obsessing, they may be lusting for pleasures, but, without a body of their own, they obsess a living person and inflict their emotions on that person so the spirit can get what they want through the living. A desire on the part of the obsessor to punish or cause suffering to someone may lead the spirit of a living person to use their relative freedom during sleep to obsess another living person. If a person dies suddenly or violently and they did not have time to prepare for their death, the spirit may get confused and continue to hover around the earth plane. It eventually finds someone with a weakened energy field and attaches itself to that person. Finally, prolonged grief for a deceased loved one may lead to the continuation of strong bonds between the living and the dead, preventing the dead from leaving the world and moving on in their spiritual evolution.

The treatment for obsession is termed disobsession in Spiritism. Disobsession helps the negatively motivated spirit, or confused spirit, to detach from the spirit which they are obsessing. This helps the obsessor to move on to their next level of soul growth. Since obsession is not good for either of the spirits involved, the process of disobsession will free them both to move on to higher levels in their spiritual evolution. Much of what happens at the Casa is disobsession work.

All are welcome at this spiritual hospital

John of God treats the rich, famous and poor. All are welcome and no one is turned away for lack of funds. People make donations, if they like, to help with Casa expenses. Additionally, John of God very generously helps the poor in the community. He has a soup kitchen for people who are hungry and he even sends some local people to college who would not otherwise be able to afford it. He makes sure that people who cannot afford the healing herbs are given the herbs they need.

Joao Teixeira de Faria is a gentle, loving soul with an extraordinary caring for humanity. Sometimes people confuse John of God – the man – with the Entities that come through him to do the healing. John of God

– Joao – is the vehicle. He often says, "I have never healed anyone. It is God who heals." The saints and doctors that come through John of God often heal when all else has failed. Western medicine and psychotherapy can fail us and sometimes people will then open to divine healing. Frequently the Casa is referred to as a "spiritual hospital." Indeed, that is a very accurate description. There are surgeries and other types of healing but the healing is always on the soul level. The mind, body and emotions heal as a side product of the deeper healing of the soul.

John of God continues to selflessly help thousands of people each week. With grace and love he helps people to heal and evolve spiritually by allowing the Entities of a higher vibration to come through his body. And, he has done this in the most extraordinary way for over five decades. To learn more about the fascinating life of John of God, I recommend the book, *The Miracle Man* by Robert Pelligrino–Estrich.

chapter 3

Miracles Abound

My first journey to John of God

Soon after I had learned that three friends had been healed by John of God, I was flying to upstate New York to see him at Omega Institute. It always felt like coming home to me when I went to Omega as I had lived many years in that area of New York and spent a lot of time at Omega. For over twenty years I had taken workshops, taught classes to the staff, and worked a couple of summers there. This time felt different as I had great hope for my deepest healing to occur. All the walkways were lined with baskets of beautiful white mums and there was a feeling of sacredness in the air.

The first night I sat down for dinner at a table with a lovely couple from Colorado Springs, Colorado. In asking what brought them to John of God, I was told an interesting story. Josh, who appeared to be in his 70's, told me that he previously had prostate cancer and that his PSA was 1200. This is unheard of! Normal is generally considered to be 5.0 or less! The doctors wanted to operate, do chemo, and all the usual Western treatments. He refused, and Josh and his wife traveled to Brazil to see John of God. They had been to Brazil a few times already. After their first visit to John of God, Josh's PSA had dropped down to 20. After the second visit it was around 5.0 and now it was 1.7. Another miracle!

Though people often come to John of God for physical healing, for me it was healing of the soul that I sought. It felt like my very soul had been invaded and wounded. My requests for the good spirits were: please stop the stalking, and help me with my trauma, depression, anxiety, insomnia, and finances. Please help me to get my life on track and make it worth living again. I had many big requests for healing.

When I first went to John of God I did not know why Richard was being so invasive and obsessive. I have come to learn that obsessive, or attached spirits, are the cause of many serious physical and psychological illnesses. This attached spirit can cause many problems for it's host. Physical, mental, emotional, and spiritual problems may result. In our culture we do not approach healing from the perspective of attached spirits. People often try everything to heal their physical, mental or emotional disorders and nothing works. It is when Western medicine and psychotherapy fail that people often become more open to soul healing. Fortunately, these spirits can be released and directed on to the next stage in their soul's journey. John of God says that most people who come to him have attached spirits and these spirits are usually the cause of the problems. Often when he helps the spirit to move on, the problem is resolved.

The disobsession work in my case took longer than the physical healings in my body. You will see, as my story goes on, that I did have some spontaneous healings and I had some that took time. Often people expect spontaneous healing when they go to John of God. Yet, we must remember that the Entities are working on the spiritual root cause of the symptoms. Sometimes the healing is spontaneous and sometimes it comes in increments. I experienced both.

Why did I create this?

This seems to be a question that a lot of people ask themselves when something goes wrong in their life. I am of the belief that we agree while we are still disin-carnate to have certain life lessons. Someone once told me that when we disincarnate we can get overly ambi-tious about what we agree to take on. We need to learn and grow to advance on a soul level. This is one reason we are here in "earth school."

Why I agreed to this particular situation I will never know! And, I don't need to know. John of God has often said, "Do you want to know what caused your cancer or do you want it healed?!" I think the same ap-proach applies to my situation. I wanted the suffering healed and I really don't need to know why this hap-pened. The root cause is what will be healed so there is no concern of it returning in some form or another.

We live in a society where we want to figure every-thing out and make sense of it all. Frequently in Boul-der you will hear people say things like, "The reason I created this breast cancer is because of my relationship with my mother!" Does it really matter why it was cre-ated if it gets healed at a soul level?! It seems to satisfy the mind in some way to make up answers but do we really know the answer to the question, "Why?"

John of God suggests that people do not ask, "Why did I create this?" If they do take that approach he most likely will not take time to answer that question. I, for one, am totally comfortable with this! Too many people judge themselves – and others – harshly for the suffering that is in their lives. It is like that comment one man made to me about the stalking, "You created it because you like it." Ouch! As if it weren't bad enough already, you just made it hurt a thousand times more.

So many angels in white

On my first full day at Omega I entered a huge white tent that could hold about 1,500 people. It was a beautiful sight to see! Hundreds of people entered the tent dressed in white, looking like angels. We had all been instructed to wear white so that the spirits that come through John of God could more easily see our energy field, our souls. Then they will know what we need for our spiritual healing.

In the front of the tent there was a stage and pictures of some of the Entities in their previous lives hanging on the wall. The volunteers on stage explained the "lines" to us. If we had never seen John of God before and have not received blessed herbs from him then we would be in the first time line. If we have had a surgery, or a spiritual intervention, from him more than eight days ago and we have not seen him for revision yet, we should go in the revision line. This is so the Entities can see how that surgery, or intervention, went and see if it is complete. Finally, someone who has seen him before but is not in the revision line, would be in the second time line. This would apply for someone seeing him for their third time, fourth time, or their hundredth time.

When the first time line was called I stood up and walked over to the line with great anticipation. Slowly the line moved and I was getting closer to the Main Hall where we would pass through two "current rooms" before we approached John of God, in–Entity. These two current rooms were filled with a few hundred people who appeared to be in a deep state of meditation. Current is similar to meditation and prayer and is two fold in its purpose. First, current is healing for the people who are sitting in current. This is where a lot of the healing takes place. Secondly, when we pray and meditate together we create a powerful energy that the Entities can use to do their healing work.

The instructions are simple when sitting in current... keep your arms and legs uncrossed and your eyes closed. I like to explain current in terms of electricity. The energy runs through everyone like electricity. The energy is amplified by many people participating and this energy helps John of God to hold the Entity in his body to do the healing work. When people sitting in current open their eyes or cross either their arms or legs they break the flow of the current. This can actually cause physical pain in John of God's body and can cause pain for the person he is operating on.

As I entered the first room filled with people sitting in current, I immediately felt a sense of deep peace and calmness. Instantly both my body and my mind relaxed and became very quiet. As I approached John of God, in–Entity, I felt the serenity go even deeper. There was a woman two people ahead of me on crutches. John of God said to one of the volunteers that was assisting him, "Take her crutches – she does not need them." They took her crutches and he told her to walk. She seemed to walk totally fine and walked for about fifteen feet before he told her to turn around and walk back. Her eyes appeared to be closed as she was walking and upon her return he said, "Now open your eyes and walk. You are healed. Go over there and sit in current."

I was mesmerized as I witnessed this, feeling like I was in a trance. To see such a miracle in front of my eyes moved something inside of me. This was just the first of countless miracles I would witness in the following years. What a blessing that the good spirits had put me here.

As I approached John of God he held his hand out and I placed my hand on his. Looking in his eyes I felt a wave of love and compassion flow into me. The Entities see us as a hologram and they know what we need for our healing. A hologram is a three dimensional image formed from light. "Holo" means whole and they see us in our entirety. Though we cannot see it, our souls are illuminated. The Entities see our energy field, our spirit. Telling them what we want is not actually necessary; though in Brazil people are still allowed to share their requests verbally as they go by John of God. I believe this is more for the comfort of the person rather than something the Entity needs to hear.

I was told to come back the following morning for a "spiritual intervention," as it is called in the United States. Here in Brazil spiritual interventions are simply called surgeries or operations. A spiritual intervention is a surgery of the soul. In the United States there are no visible surgeries where John of God cuts into a person with a knife or performs other types of physical surgeries.

The interpreter told me to take the afternoon to prepare for the intervention so I decided to make an appointment for a crystal bed treatment. I was totally curious about these beds. The images in my mind consisted of me lying on hundreds of crystals with their tips pointed up; rather like a yogi lying on a bed of nails. Fortunately, that is not how it was!

My crystal bed experience

As I entered the darkened room I was taken to a massage table. What a relief that was! I laid down and a small towel was placed over my eyes. The attendant adjusted seven crystals that were above me so they would shine light on each of my seven chakras or energy centers in my body. Each crystal had the corresponding color of the chakra shining through and the lights flashed on and off throughout the session which lasted about half an hour.

The best way to describe my experience was that it was like taking a good trip on acid! I was floating in and out of my body and was fully conscious the entire time. Being a very visual person, there were explosions of color, and a multitude of images as I travelled through time and space. I love the crystal bed experience!

Everyone has different experiences on the crystal beds and yours might be very different from mine. But, what we all have in common is that our energy fields are being opened up. This makes it easier for the Entities to do their work and to go deeper with it. Whatever we can do to open and prepare ourselves for their healing makes their work more effective.

It didn't feel like lightning bolts... what could have possibly happened!?

The next morning Medium Joao "incorporated" on stage before treating the hundreds of people that were waiting to see him. This is the moment the saint or other healing spirit comes into his body and

Medium Joao loses consciousness. I watched with total fascination as a person on each side of him held his hands. He shuddered as the spirit came into his body. Now John of God was "in–Entity." He seemed to grow bigger and he held his body differently. His features and his expression changed in front of our eyes. Even his voice changed. His presence seemed bigger than life. It was amazing to watch and feel what was happening right in front of us. I was deeply moved and felt so very blessed.

Now the consciousness of John of God, the man, will enter into a sleep–like state until he disincorporates at the end of the session. He will not remember anything of what goes on during this time. If he sees you when he is disincorporated he will not remember your interaction. Even if he performed a surgery on you, he will not remember. After incorporation, John of God walked back to the room where he would see and treat people.

When the spiritual intervention line was called I walked with the others that had been called for an intervention. First we passed through the current rooms and once again I felt showered with peace and love. My whole being relaxed. Thinking that my intervention would be one on one with John of God, I was very surprised to learn that I would be in a room with about a hundred and fifty other people. We were all to receive our intervention at the same time and my mind thought,

"What could possibly happen with so many of us?"

I sat down on a chair that I was directed to and held a crystal of mine in my hand with a piece of paper wrapped around it. On this paper I had written my requests. We had been told that the Entities can work on up to nine requests during an intervention. My roommate, Marianne, and I were overjoyed when we heard this! We had thought it was only three. So, the night before we had sat in our cabin and made our lists of the nine things we would like healed in our lives.

Since I now had room for nine requests I added a couple of physical things to my list... nothing life threatening... but I had room for more requests. The first request was for the healing of a 3-centimeter lump in my breast. The lump had been with me for many years. When I was about 14 one of my sisters lunged at me unexpectedly, pinched my breast as hard as anyone could, and twisted her hand while pinching. The pain was so intense I felt myself blacking out and there was no fighting back. I was just in shock. Sometimes she did these things out of the blue and my mom dismissed them saying she just has a "mean streak" and she could not help it. When I was about twenty a very hard solid mass was discovered where she had attacked me. I just let it be, considering the mass to be some sort of karmic thing, and it never grew any bigger over the following decades.

The second physical request I had was for the healing of low back pain. The pain had been with me for about four months. While hiking in the Rocky Mountains I had turned my head to the left to talk with a friend behind me. Then my right foot slipped on some gravel and I wrenched my back pretty severely. I had had low back pain ever since that incident.

As we sat in the intervention room the leaders gave us instructions. They said to keep our arms and legs uncrossed and to absolutely keep our eyes closed during the spiritual intervention. If we did not do this we would be breaking the current of energy that flows through us. They informed us that the intervention may last just a few minutes or it may go on for hours. John of God would be there with us until all our prayers were answered.

I heard John of God come into the room and listened to his voice for what seemed like just a couple of minutes. Then I heard his footsteps as he walked out of the room. Someone translated and said that the Entity proclaimed, "All my children are healed." We were then instructed to go outside to receive our post–intervention instructions. As I opened my eyes I remember thinking, "I feel good but what could possibly have happened?! A hundred and fifty people... two minutes! It certainly wasn't lightning bolts!"

I walked to the tent with the other people to receive instructions. For the next 24 hours we were to remain in bed and sleep if we were tired. If we didn't feel tired we should pretend we are sleeping and keep our eyes closed. John of God's assistants reminded us that this was a powerful intervention even if we didn't realize it, and that we should treat it as such.

This first 24 hours is a very delicate and vulnerable time. A person's energy field is totally wide open as the spirits are working at a soul level for healing. It is not a time to intermingle our energies with others. Friends who had not had an intervention brought me food so that I could stay in bed during this time.

The spirits yelled at me!

As I lay in my bed in our cabin I felt slightly energized but I closed my eyes. Then I thought about that lump in my breast and my hand automatically went to that spot to feel it and see if it was smaller. But, I couldn't find it! I started poking around as my mind was sure it had to still be there... at least partially. Though I knew where it had been located, after living with it for decades, I searched elsewhere going deeper to find it. Then I heard a firm, clear and loud voice that said, "STOP POKING AND PRODDING! YOU JUST HAD SURGERY!"

Instantly I pulled my hand away and thought "Whoa!" I felt like I had been scolded by the spirits! I believe it was Dr. Augusto... one of the spirits that commonly comes through. His personality is sometimes sharp and he is very direct. I placed my hand very gently on my right breast and apologized to my breast saying, "I'm sorry... I hope I didn't hurt you." Finally, I drifted off to sleep.

The next day I shared the story with Marianne. She always tells me how she hears "quiet, little voices of the spirits" that talk to her. I said to her, "They YELLED at me!!! The spirits yelled at me!" And, we had a good laugh.

I learned a couple of big lessons from the lump spontaneously disappearing. First, I learned that anything in the universe can change instantly. This gives me great hope for us Earthlings getting out of the mess we are in! I also learned that change can be beyond what we believe is possible. I did not believe that this lump could simply disappear... that is why I was poking and prodding... I simply could not believe it. Though I had heard of spontaneous healing, until I experienced it, I never really "got it." Now, I got it! Many people say that these healings occur because people believe they will occur. In my experience, although belief may be helpful, it is not absolutely necessary. I can imagine even a skeptic being healed as long as they follow the protocols.

Back pain gone forever

My low back pain was gone and never returned after that day. It seemed that the physical healings were easier to take care of with me. I wondered if the spirits did that as a sign to let me know that they are working. After all, the other things were not physical. The less tangible requests would need to be watched more closely. These physical healings helped me to know that the spirits were there working on me and that this was all real.

I had a second intervention just a few days later. This one was much more difficult for me. It felt like the spirits were pulling tentacles out of my energetic field. This is the best way I can describe the images. They were pulling the tentacles of Richard out and it was a hard pull. It was like he was in my field and sucking my life energy out of me. The life energy he sucked fed him and gave him energy. As they pulled and tugged they got the sucking tentacles out and closed up the holes so that no unwanted energies could enter.

My traumatic ordeal is at the beginning of the end

When I returned home I immediately started sleeping well. This, after two and a half years of feeling attacked at night. I know that Richard had been brutally attacking me on a psychic level in the middle of the night. It was very disturbing to my sleep and to my psyche. Now, finally that was done. I was amazed... and eternally grateful.

Another very obvious change occurred with this first visit. People who commit crimes like Richard often have patterns. It seems to be a part of their game. Their pattern is known and very identifiable by the person being victimized. Without revealing the pattern that marked his crimes I will say that his pattern was broken with my first visit to John of God. It was obvious to me and I knew this was the beginning of the end of this ordeal. He made contact only once after my first visit to John of God... about six months later.

Although I did receive those two spontaneous physical healings with my first visit, and my insomnia disappeared, my full recovery took several visits. With each subsequent visit, I made significant progress and seeing that certainly kept me going. We live in a society where people often want quick fixes and they want someone else to do their healing for them. Yet, when we are dealing with the very source of the dis-ease – rather than just making symptoms disappear – it can be a longer process. I understood this and certainly was willing to go the full hundred yards.

chapter 4

A Fun and Playful Journey

Can my family handle my latest spiritual quest?

My healing journey had finally begun. It was a long journey but knowing that the spirits were working with me was a huge help. I had made a connection with the spirit world that I had never known before and this connection would continue to grow stronger and stronger over the years. I never felt alone again.

I went to visit my mom in upstate New York before going to see John of God for my second visit. Though I was raised in the Catholic religion I felt this might be a bit beyond what my family could handle. For decades

I had been exploring all sorts of paths to help me to understand what life is all about. They had endured many phases of my growth!

My first communal experience was in the '70s when I became involved at a yoga ashram. I remember my mother being concerned as she warned me to not drink any Kool-Aid! Eventually, yoga became very acceptable in our society and then my mom would say, "You were just always a little bit ahead of everyone else."

Then I became a disciple of Bhagwan Rajneesh (now "Osho") in the early 80's and my family watched me wearing red clothes and mala beads. Osho had given me the name Sujato, meaning well born with truth and clarity, which I still use in many circles. Though often misunderstood and mis-quoted, Osho was brilliant. He died in 1990 but I still love doing His meditations and listening to what He had to say.

Now this! Oh, my goodness! Could my family handle yet another spiritual quest I was diving into!? The first time I went to visit John of God I simply said to my family, "I'm going to a meditation retreat." They were used to hearing that from me and it seemed to be something that was easily digested. I left it at that!

Now as I headed to my second visit to see John of God at Omega I got braver! First, I told my mom, since she has had many spiritual and paranormal experiences throughout her life. She was completely accepting of my newest spiritual quest so I asked her if she would like me to request healing for her and she responded, "Yes!"

When a person cannot go directly to John of God for some reason they can request distance healing; sometimes called remote healing. This is done by bringing the person's photo, along with some information and requests on the back, to John of God. The photo stays near him in a very strong healing field for one year. I took a picture of my mom and she wrote her requests for help on the back.

Her primary request was for help with her heart. Since my dad died in 2001, my mom was having very disturbing heart palpitations at night. Sometimes her heartbeat would be very fast and sometimes very irregular as it skipped beats. It happened every single night, and she was tired from her sleep being so disturbed.

Several weeks later, after I had returned from John of God, I talked to my mom and she said, "I forgot to tell you... when you delivered my photo to John of God the irregular heartbeat stopped! It has been totally fine ever since and it's no longer keeping me awake at night!" Now, about five years later, her heartbeat is still totally fine.

The good spirits laugh and play with me!

My second visit was very different from the first. In fact, every visit has been very unique. I did not receive any interventions on my second visit and the Entities were totally playful with me every time I went by them. It was fun!

On this visit each time I approached John of God the Entity looked me straight in the eye and had the biggest smile imaginable! One time he reached his hand out towards me with his palm up and as I went to place my hand on his I noticed the most perfect little rosebud that I had ever seen. I looked up at him and communicated non-verbally, "Am I supposed to take this?" With a big smile he nodded his head yes.

Another day when I passed by him he had a delightful childlike energy about him. Someone about four people ahead of me had given him a bouquet of daisies. He again was looking me in the eye with a big smile as he handed me one of the daisies in a way that said, "Oh, boy! This is fun! Let's play! Let's connect! Here's a flower... we are friends!" It obviously put a big smile on my face to see and feel this energy. This undoubtedly was the happiest smile I had experienced in over three years.

I recall walking by him one time on this visit and I did not see John of God's face. I saw someone else's face. He had very big eyes and a full, round face. I did not think much of it until two months later when I saw a photo of one of the Entities named Dr. Valdivino. It was him! This was the person I had seen! What a fun discovery to know who this playful person was!

The Entities all have their own personalities so your experience can be very different each time you walk by John of God. Often when passing by John of God, in–Entity, he will be looking at someone who is four people behind you. I always tell people to not take this personally! The Entities are scanning the souls of people behind you in line and seeing the past, present and future within each spirit. It is through seeing this that they know how to treat each individual for their best healing. The fun, light, playful energy that they greeted me with on this second visit is not always how I am greeted. Some of the Entities are much more serious.

Two cups of coffee

On my second day during this visit the assistants asked if anyone would like to sit in current. They needed more people in there to hold the energy. I thought to myself, "Darn, I shouldn't have had those two cups of coffee at breakfast!" It is expected that when you sit in current you stay there and don't break the current.

This could be three, four or five hours that you are sitting. In spite of this, I found myself leaping out of my seat and heading to the current room.

Instantly when I sat down my body became very heavy. We sat for about three hours and it felt like forty minutes. Not once did I think about the need to go to the bathroom. It was a visual experience as I floated through time, space, and swirling colors. When it was time to open my eyes my body was so heavy that it was hard to move. I felt like I had elephant legs! Initially, I had to lift my legs to move them!

I love sitting in current! Though I have meditated for over three decades, I have always had a hard time sitting for extended periods of time. For me one hour was an "extended period of time"! But, this very first time in current, I was in such a deeply altered state that the hours flew by. My healing was deep and I was happy to know that I was assisting John of God in doing his work.

As my healing journey continued I began to chart my symptoms just like I ask my patients to do. As a biofeedback therapist I work primarily with chronic pain and headache patients and I have them rank their symptoms daily so that we have an accurate record of their improvement. Since I was not asking for healing of anything physical, I wanted a detailed record so I could truly see what was going on. Using a scale of one to ten I ranked various symptoms such as depression, crying, sadness, overwhelm, anxiety, etc. Every time I went to John of God my symptoms got better and better. There had been a time when these symptoms of trauma were all up close to ten.

The stalking stopped three years after it had begun. During that time I had nothing to do with men and did not know if I could trust a man again. Now it was time to test the waters and see if I could connect with a man again. Would I be able to love and trust a man again? Would I be able to have a healthy relationship again? Was I permanently damaged? These are the thoughts that went through my mind.

A few months later I became involved with a man I shall call Jim. Jim was retired and we had a lot of fun together. Fun, laughter and lightness was definitely the order of the day. Jim had a great sense of humor and it was all perfect for me at the time. For a couple of years we played and travelled together, spending time in Thailand and other great places. We did many wonderful things that lifted my spirits.

One night Jim had a special date planned for me. I could not imagine what the occasion was but soon I found out that it was my "half-birthday"! Jim handed me a half-birthday card and inside was a gift certificate saying that I could chose where our next trip was going to be! I was ecstatic! And, of course, he knew the next trip would be to Brazil... specifically Abadiania!

chapter 5

To Brazil We Go!

My journey to Abadiania

Jim was a total skeptic but he was good spirited about going to see John of God since he had given me the choice. We spent a week in Rio and then were off for a two week stay in Abadiania before traveling elsewhere. As we headed to Abadiania he said, "I might go traveling for those two weeks and come back and meet you if I can't handle this." I was fine with that as I knew this was not his thing.

I had arranged for a guide on this first trip because there is much that will be missed without guidance. She handled all of our logistical details, reserved a wonderful place for us to stay at, answered all of our questions and guided us every step of the way. Without a guide we would have been spending much of our time trying to figure everything out and I was ready to focus all of my attention on my healing. I highly recommend that you use a guide on your first visit and concentrate on what you are really going for.

As we landed in Brasilia there was excitement stirring within me. After proceeding through customs, it was a welcome sight to see a man holding a sign that said, "Kelsie and Jim." Our guide had arranged to have our taxi waiting there for us as we walked out into the beautiful open-air terminal. I greeted him with, "Bom dia! Eu sou Kelsie!" (Good day! I am Kelsie!)... and off we went!

After a one and a half hour taxi ride we arrived at our pousada, or guesthouse. Our room was beautiful and I was very impressed by everything... the delicious food, the beautiful gardens, and the love that went into every detail on the part of the cooks, cleaners, and the management. This is a very special pousada and it certainly was a supportive environment for deep healing to occur.

The House of Love

Later that night we walked over to the Casa and got our first glimpse. Instantly I felt bathed in the love and peace that permeates the air at the Casa. It is indeed a house of love. When I say that the Casa is a house of love, I speak on a couple of levels. There is human love and divine love. Both can be found at the Casa and both help with the healing. On the human level we can feel people loving themselves and each other far more than we experience it in Western society. This human love truly feeds the soul.

The divine love comes from our Creator, from Source. We can feel ourselves being flooded with this divine love when we see Joao in–Entity... or it can be in current... it can take us over anywhere. Witnessing a visible surgery is a physical event that assures us of the presence of divine love. God is unquestionably there. You cannot doubt God when you witness these operations.

The grounds feel exquisitely sacred at the Casa. It is located at the edge of town with gently rolling hills and distant views. Lush greenery filled the views on my first visit and there were many tropical birds sing-ing their songs. The Casa is on a very sacred piece of land that fosters healing. There is a strong and power-ful force field here. It is built on a huge bed of crystals that, undoubtedly, adds to the amped up energy here. The vibration of decades of healing work is held in the physical manifestation of the Casa. With a sensation of paradise abounding I instantly felt deeply relaxed and at home here.

As we took our tour through the Casa we first come to the bookstore. Books, blessed water, crystals and other items are sold here. There are many kinds of crystals available and all of the crystals that are sold here have been blessed by the Entities. The Casa crystals carry a very strong energy... more potent and healing than I have ever felt in a crystal before.

Next we passed the cafe which offers snacks and fresh coconut water... yum! Then we entered a room that was filled with canes, crutches and wheelchairs that were cast off by people who no longer needed them. In the next room there was a locked cabinet with jars in it that contained tumors and body parts that had been removed during physical surgeries. We were told about one woman who had cancer throughout her whole body. The Entity told her that if she was willing to loose one part of her body He would pull all of the cancer to that part – to her little finger – and cut it off. She agreed and was healed of her cancer. Her little finger remains in a jar in this cabinet. We then completed our tour with a walk through the assembly hall, gardens, soup area and ended our tour at the meditation deck just in time for a magnificent sunset over the beautiful rolling hills.

Medium Joao is at the Casa on Wednesday, Thursday, and Friday of each week to do healing work on the thousands of people that travel from around the globe to see him. John of God prefers to be called Medium Joao and now that I am in Brazil I find myself referring to him this way.

The Casa, or "house," is named after St. Dom Inacio de Loyola who was the founder of the Jesuit order. He was a great healer in his day and he is one of the Entities that comes through when the current is very strong. We are told that his energy is very subtle and it is difficult for Medium Joao to hold in his body. Dom Inacio de Loyola does not come through often, but, when he does the healings are even stronger and more profound than on other days. We are also told that Dom Inacio de Loyola will not be coming through much longer because his spirit is getting too fine and thin for Medium Joao to hold in his body.

I watch my first "visible surgery"

As we headed off to the Casa on our first Wednesday in Abadiania we joined dozens of people dressed in white walking down the middle of the road in the morning sun. It was a beautiful sight. There were many people in wheelchairs and many others had visible impairments. Sick children were being brought and that tugged at my heart. Most people, including myself, had nothing visible on the outside. Though it seems that most come here for physical healing, I would imagine that many come for healing of trauma, depression, anxiety and other disorders that can be just as devastating but not visible to the naked eye.

We gathered in the assembly hall to wait for the morning session to begin. Up front there is a small stage where Medium Joao, in–Entity, performs the visible surgeries. One of the Casa volunteers got up onto the stage and asked us to raise our hands if we were to be in the first time line. She took a count and then she did the same for all of the other lines. This is very important so they can monitor Medium Joao's energy in order to keep his physical body healthy. Allowing these spirits to come in to do their work is a big strain on his physical body.

We then prayed and listened to people share stories on stage as we waited for our line to be called. The people who were invited for surgery go in first to be with Medium Joao. Once they sit down someone says to them, "If there is anyone here who is over 18 and under 52 and would like a visible surgery, please stand up now and follow me." They are asked a few simple questions and then, with no anesthesia given, they are taken to the stage for their physical operation. The stage is in the assembly hall and people are free to take photos and videos there. It is quite an amazing sight to see and to this day I am always moved by witnessing these surgeries.

The first visible surgery I witnessed was of a woman having a lump removed from her breast. The woman was standing and leaning against a wall with her eyes closed. She seemed totally at peace. I watched as Medium Joao cut into her breast with a knife. He then stuck his fingers inside her, without any gloves, and pulled out what appeared to be a tumor. It has been proven over and over that the tissue he removes does come from the person he is operating on. It is not "slight of hand" as I was sure it was when I saw that television show years ago!

I have to admit it made me squeamish watching this surgery. Yet, this woman was peaceful as though she were having a wonderful sleep. Clearly, I was more disturbed by the surgery than she was! Then there are other times when I watch with total curiosity and amazement and I know that I must be in some sort of relaxed trance state as I watch Medium Joao cut into someone's flesh.

During this visit I was able to witness many visible surgeries. Though Medium Joao says they are absolutely not necessary he continues to do them to increase our faith… and that it does! To witness people being cut, tumors being yanked on and pulled out, and to see people stitched up without feeling any pain is miraculous. You realize there is a whole lot more going on here than meets the eye. In addition to not feeling pain, people bleed very little considering the incisions and there has never been a reported case of infection. When watching these surgeries you know that, without a doubt, God is orchestrating this.

I have witnessed Medium Joao, in–Entity, do many eye scrapings. During these procedures he takes a kitchen knife, sometimes with a serrated edge, and scraps the eyeball and cornea. He does this hard enough that I have witnessed the indent on the eyeball and the sound of the knife scraping. Under normal conditions people would be screaming in pain. The eye scraping can be used to heal many disorders and they need not have anything to do with the eyes.

The "nose job," as it is affectionately called, is another common procedure. This is also used for a variety of disorders and can cure many disorders at the same time. The concerns may have nothing to do with the respiratory tract or the brain. Medium Joao, in–Entity, asks the patient to lean their head back slightly. He then takes a hemostat (an instrument that looks like long, slender scissors) which is about seven inches in length and shoves it up the nostril quickly. Often he twists it around and sometimes he leaves it in for a bit of time before removing it. It is abrupt and quite shocking to see. After he removes the hemostat the patient is taken in a wheelchair to the recovery room.

The recovery room, or infirmary, is a room with beds where all people who have had a physical surgery go to rest. They are lovingly watched after by Casa volunteers as their spiritual anesthesia wears off. This is, as it's name suggests, an anesthesia that is given by the spirits so the patient does not feel pain. There is no physical anesthesia given for any of the procedures. It can take a couple of hours for this spiritual anesthesia to wear off. When the patient comes to a more conscious state, they take a taxi back to their pousada to rest in bed for a minimum of twenty-four hours.

Witnessing the physical surgeries will likely challenge your belief system as they defy what we know scientifically and medically. I think this is a good thing! It opens us to a reality of which we know very little. Sometimes we like to think we know it all. These surgeries show us in a tangible way that God is present. There is no other explanation. We are witnessing miracles and that is life altering.

Disappearing into the triangle

After that first morning session I took some photos of loved ones to a large wooden triangle on the wall behind the stage. Hundreds of thousands of visitors have prayed there over the years and it is a very powerful spot. People are free to leave photos in the triangle and pray for the healing of others. A long, oblong brown mark shows where countless people have laid their foreheads into the triangle over the decades.

I had my mom's photo with me and I placed it in the triangle. Then, putting my head forward to touch the wall, I immediately felt like I was transported to a deep, holy, and silent place. I connected with the Entities and asked them to help my mom. She needed to get into an assisted living home quickly but there was over a six month wait to get into a nice home. When I left for Brazil she told me, "Please ask them to help me quickly with this." Miraculously, she was moved into an amazing assisted living home within one month's time! She knew the good spirits had their hands in this!

The sacred waterfall

One of the treatments for healing is purification by the sacred waterfall and a person must get permission from the Entities before going there. My first visit to the sacred waterfall... cachoeira in Portuguese... was to be cherished. I walked alongside my guide down a beautiful dirt road for about a half mile past the Casa. When we reached the area where taxis park, we paused in silence, saying a prayer to the good spirits and letting our requests be known. I could already feel the sacredness of the waterfall at this point.

We then proceeded in silence down a narrow path. Walking slowly, and focusing on each step, I kept my awareness on my intentions and requests. The path took us to a sitting area where people wait their turn to go down to the waterfall. As I sat and waited, I felt as though I was in a jungle paradise. Everything was lush green and spectacular butterflies flittered by. They were of varied and bright colors. Listening to the sounds of the waterfall in the background, I felt like I was in a land of magic.

Finally, it was our turn and I went down with four other women. Men and women generally go separately as prescribed by the Entities. Leaving our clothes and bags on a bench, we began our approach towards the falls in our bathing suits. Walking slowly, I could feel nature spirits all around. Everything felt vibrantly alive around me as I walked gingerly over a wooden bridge to approach the falls.

It felt like a whole different world down there as I approached the waterfall. Slowly I made my way towards the falls maneuvering the slippery rocks with care. Then, standing underneath the falls I began to place my head under the cold water. The pounding of the cold water on my head and shoulders felt so good! I never would have imagined cold water to feel so good! It was as though it were washing my spirit and sending any unhealthy energy down the river. As it cleansed me I could feel the purification.

After a couple of minutes I walked from the falls, feeling like I had been given new life. My requests had been for clarity, strength, and protection. And, I knew within myself that my prayers had been answered. There was a surge of energy that went through me as I walked up to the bench and then said a prayer of gratitude to the Entities for listening... and for helping me.

I have been to the sacred waterfall many times since this first visit. To this day, every time I go it is as powerful, magical and mystical as my very first experience. The spirits are, without a doubt, busy working there... assisting us with our healing. It is an integral part of the treatment for many people.

The many medicines

In addition to the waterfalls there are many other treatments used to assist in a person's healing at the Casa. Some of the treatments – invisible surgery, visible surgery, sitting in current, and crystal beds – I have already talked about. In addition to these treatments, consuming the blessed soup and water help with a person's healing.

The energization of water has long been used as medicine for spirit and body. If you are familiar with Masaru Emoto's work you know that he spent many years researching the molecular structure of water under various circumstances. He found that the molecular structure of water can be changed by the thoughts and intentions put on the water. Water at the Casa is blessed by the saints and other spirits that come through Medium Joao. When we drink this blessed water, or eat the blessed soup, we are ingesting medicine into our bodies which are over 90% water. The blessed soup is considered part of the protocol for healing and is served every Wednesday, Thursday, and Friday after the morning session.

All of these treatments help to open up our energy fields allowing us to access higher vibrations for healing. This opening can leave the patient vulnerable to external energies that might not be beneficial. You can imagine the importance of being alone in bed for twenty four hours following surgery when one's field is very open. All of the protocols at the Casa were put forth by the Entities and should be followed carefully for optimal healing.

All the courageous people

It takes a very special kind of person to be attracted enough to the work of Medium Joao that they disrupt their life to journey across the globe. There was a courageous young woman at our pousada on this visit. She had multiple sclerosis and just a couple of years ago she was in a wheelchair. Twice a year she comes here from England with her mom and her boyfriend. Her boyfriend wanted to marry her but she said that she would not do that to him; adding that when she could walk on her own they would get engaged. On this visit she was walking with a walker and they were engaged!

Some people may think that this is a place full of sadness and disease. On the contrary, it is a place full of love, hope, and miracles.

Annie

Among the many wonderful people Jim and I met on our trip was Annie McGuire. Annie is a lively person who was staying in the same pousada we were. She is a medium who communicates with spirits of the deceased. People come to her when they want to communicate with a relative, friend, or lover that has passed on. She is a different kind of medium from Medium Joao.

Medium Joao is a "full trance medium." This means that he is not conscious when the good spirits come in to use his body for the healings. He feels like he is sleeping and he does not remember a thing. Annie, on the other hand, is fully conscious when she communicates with spirits on the other side.

One day Annie came down to breakfast very excited. She lifted up her shirt a bit and there was a huge blister that ran around her ribcage. It was about a foot long and was very pronounced. She had felt it in the shower and was surprised at what she saw... a visible surgery that occurred when Medium Joao was not around and no one was in current. Apparently she had been in the assembly hall the day before and suddenly she felt like she needed to lie down. As she lay on a bench, her right arm was up exposing her ribcage underneath. She had felt like she had taken a short nap. This, she said, is when it happened.

Annie initially wondered what the surgery was for but she quickly realized that it is futile to try to make sense of anything here! In the afternoon the blister broke, there was a small amount of blood, and it all scabbed up forming a very long scab around her ribcage. Needless to say, Jim's eyes were opening as he witnessed this all firsthand.

The spirits were starting to get hold of Jim in Abadiania! He was sitting in current at least once a day and he was more relaxed and happy than I had ever seen him. Contentment filled his aura and he was enjoying the people, the food, and sitting in current. And, this was a man who previously could not meditate to save his life.

Spontaneous invisible operations like Annie experienced happen quite frequently. Sometimes they leave a physical mark and sometimes they do not. After returning from this trip I had an unexpected operation the very day after my return. I was in my condo and suddenly I felt knocked out and like I had to lie down immediately. But, I didn't lie down because I was resisting that and at first I did not know what was going on. I continued to unpack and do things in spite of feeling very weak. Almost immediately I got a bloody nose which was unusual for me. I thought that maybe it was due to the dry weather in Colorado, although that was not normal for me. Soon I realized that the blood was not coming from just inside my nose. It was coming from way up high in the nasal passage.

I still did not understand what was going on! Then, finally, the spirits said to me, "You just had surgery!" Oh, there were those words once again! Sometimes I feel a little slow when I don't get what's going on until the spirits say it to me loud and clear. I responded with, "Oh, NO! Not the nose job!" I immediately went to bed for twenty four hours and followed the protocols.

I do realize that this sounds like crazy, insane stuff. In fact, I hesitated to even share this last story with you. There was a day when people got locked up for

saying this kind of thing. But, I am of the attitude...
"Whatever works!" – and the healing that comes
through Medium Joao undoubtedly works.

Spirits in my photos

I took many photos on my first visit to the Casa as
everything was so fascinating to me. In general visitors are allowed to take photos anywhere on the Casa
property except in the current rooms. I took photos of
people in the Assembly Hall and I took videos of the
visible surgeries that were performed on stage.

I noticed something very interesting when I got
back to my room in the pousada and uploaded the photos to my computer. The people in some of the photos
looked surreal. They looked flat and translucent. It
was as though you could see right through them. There
were shafts of white light radiating vertically through
the photo and through the people. In one of the photos, a man in the middle was out of focus but the other
people in the photo were in focus. This photo was also
filled with white light streaming through the people in
a vertical manner.

I can assure you that there was nothing wrong
with my camera! In fact, most of the photos looked normal. This shows me, in a very physical way, the powerful spirit energies that are at work here. The phalange

of spirits are quite busy in the Assembly Hall as we gather. Our healing is being supported long before we walk in front of Medium Joao.

The following year I took a video of a physical surgery that showed light around Medium Joao and the person he was operating on. Every day for the next three weeks I went into the hall at that time to see if there was a possibility that this light could be coming through the fans above on the wall. You know the mind wants to make sense of this! Though the lights did look like light coming through the fans, the positioning of the light was clearly distorted. In these videos the light hovered around Medium Joao and the person he was operating on.

The toll on Medium Joao

This work is physically exhausting for Medium Joao. He has total dedication to his mission but he is human, after all. One day a friend of mine wanted to get her photo taken with Medium Joao and we waited outside of his office to see if he might come out. When he opened the door and I saw his face I was deeply concerned. I hesitated and my thoughts were, "Oh, my gosh... go to bed... get help..." He had worked to help with the healing of hundreds of people that hot day.

Medium Joao saw my hesitation as I did not move from the bench. But, he also saw my friend's camera and he graciously waved us into his office. Then I thought, "How could he wave us in when he looks so drained?" He is an extraordinarily giving man. Rarely do I show anyone the photo of that day... unless I want them to really understand how this work affects him.

That day greatly impacted me and I see how important it is for all of us to support him however we can. I hold him in light and say prayers for him. I hold him in my meditations and have him on my altar. Whenever I think of him I send good energy his way and I encourage others to do the same. Every week now on Thursday night people around the globe pray for him at 9 PM their time. You are, of course, invited to say your own prayers of support for the health of Medium Joao.

The taxi driver in the black suit

The Entities continued to work on Jim though he would probably say that he stayed two full weeks because he liked the food at our pousada! Now in our second week in Abadiania we had to decide what we would do with our final week in Brazil. For the past six months Jim made me promise that we would be no longer than ten days here and we were already here two weeks. There was no way that I could suggest a third week here. Then a miracle happened! Jim suggested that we stay here for our final week! I could hardly believe my ears!

During our third week Jim went in front of Medium Joao with a photo of a friend who was very ill. He had been told not to go in line unless he was open to healing for himself. But, he did go, and back in the room he said to me, "I am doing a surrogate surgery tomorrow for Carol." After asking him a few questions I told him that I thought the operation was intended for him, and I asked if he had gotten a prescription for herbs for Carol. He said, "No, John of God handed me her photo back with this paper... with a scribble and a dot on it!" Then I said, "That is a prescription for Carol and the operation is for YOU!" "How do you know that is a prescription?!" he said, to which I responded, "Obviously this is a prescription! Look at it!" We both had a good laugh and now he knows what a prescription looks like.

He insisted that he would not go for the operation because he said he is perfect just the way he is and he did not want anything to be healed. The Entities will not work on someone unless they have permission. We do have free will and choice. We must give God permission to heal us if that is what we want. Since Jim did not want any healing, the Entities would not interfere with that. Perhaps it was enough for him to have witnessed all the paranormal phenomena that had come into his life during his visit. If he is ready for healing at a later time the Entities will be there to help him when he requests it.

The following morning after breakfast I set a cup of tea up on a shelf of a bureau in our room. A drawer below the shelf was open with Jim's things in it. He asked me if I was going to leave my tea there and when I responded with a "yes" he closed his drawer so the tea would not accidentally spill in there.

Less that two minutes later we were standing about three feet from the bureau and I was lightly teasing him when I said, "So, are you going to your surgery this morning!?" When he responded in the negative we instantly heard a very loud noise from the bureau and a rattling of things in the drawer. We simultaneously looked over and the drawer had jumped out about seven inches!

Jim said, "I just closed that! I know I closed that because of your tea! Didn't I just close that!?" I said, "Yes... I think the spirits are talking to you! They are telling you to go to your surgery!" Jim was a little spooked by this and later he told me that he had never in his life had anything paranormal happen to him. I was shocked to hear that because I have had paranormal events occur throughout my life. It surprised me to know that someone could live for so long without something out of the ordinary happening.

We both checked the drawer to see what amount of force that it took for the drawer to jump out. It was an old bureau with warped wood and great force was needed for this to happen. After checking the drawer Jim sat down on the bed and pulled his computer out and he became very quiet. He was attempting to finish watching a DVD he had started the day before, but, it simply would not work. He put the DVD in four times. Finally, on the fourth attempt he got the visual but no sound. The volume was turned up on both the DVD player and on his computer.

He told me what was going on and his mind could not grasp what was happening. Again I teased him and said, "They are telling you to get off your computer and go to your surgery!" Then he set his computer aside and curled up in a fetal position. I could tell this was all getting to be a little much for him and I stopped my teasing.

Later, at lunch, he mentioned that the surgery was scheduled for the afternoon. Sometimes the Entities want you to see a particular doctor or saint that will be there for a certain session. When he told me this I said, "Oh, you didn't tell me you were scheduled for the afternoon! You still have time to go!" to which he responded, "I am not going to the surgery but I want to sit in current. Will you come with me?" I told him that I would be happy to sit in current with him.

I intuitively knew that something was going to happen that afternoon but I did not know what. A lot can happen in the current room. It is extremely powerful sitting in current. Off we went to be in current for about three and a half hours. When we came out I asked him if he would mind waiting for a moment while I put someone's photo in the triangle for healing. He said that was fine and he sat down on a bench in the assembly hall. I approached the triangle behind the stage and my back was to him for about two or three minutes.

We left the hall and began walking down the street when he said to me, "You won't believe what happened in there!" I looked at him and his face was all lit up like a Christmas tree. Jim had a huge smile and he was just beaming with energy. Now you have to understand that this man is a big jokester. He has a great sense of humor and he knows how to keep people laughing. I responded with, "Oh, I can't wait to hear this one!" as I was as fully expecting to hear some outrageous spoof.

He said, "No, really!" After a bit I began to see that he was serious... something had happened to him in there... and he began to tell his story. A man in a black suit came up to him, he said, while I was up at the triangle. The man said something to him but he could not hear it so he stood up and the man whispered in his ear, "Francisco?" Jim shook his head to say "no" and he sat back down. This tall man in the black suit then went into the current room with a piece of paper in his hand, according to Jim. Jim, still all lit up, said, "I just thought it was interesting, given all the paranormal things that are happening today, that he asked if I was Francisco. My parents almost gave me that name because I was born on October 4 and St. Francis is my patron saint."

Then, very quickly, Jim tried to rationalize what happened and he said, "But I am sure he was a taxi driver because he had that paper in his hand and he was looking for Francisco!" I said, "Isn't it a little unusual for a taxi driver to be wearing a black suit in the summer time in Brazil!?" Jim had to admit that it was! Then I added, "And, isn't it a little odd that he went into the current room after it was over and no one was in there?" Yes, Jim admitted that was odd, too. "And what about the fact that there is a line for the taxi drivers to wait in outside the hall and they don't come in to look for people?" I inquired. Things just didn't add up!

I knew that Jim had seen a spirit. That happens here. It has never happened to me... the spirits talk to me but I have never seen one. I certainly do not know who that spirit was but my gut tells me that it was a relative of Jim's. The spirit talked as though he was from Sicily and that is where Jim's family was from. The next morning Jim checked his computer and now it was working just fine. He flew out later that morning to the Galapagos Islands to do some traveling on his own. I went to the assembly hall where they happened to announce the Entity that was present the previous afternoon. Typically, it is not announced who the Entity is that comes through. They always say that it truly does not matter... we don't need to know. But, on this morning they did announce who was there yesterday afternoon. Indeed, it was Saint Francis, Jim's patron saint!

chapter 6

Home Again, Home Again

My ankle heals... my back adjusts... healing's happening everywhere!

Whenever I would return back home after being with Medium Joao my connection would still be strong. The spirits would be very close by and I was now able to call on them directly. It was as though I had developed a clear channel to the good spirits... the Entities of Medium Joao.

One time I was at a restaurant in Boulder with a group of friends for my birthday. The place was quite dark and I had walked up a few steps to ask something of one of the waiters. We got into a friendly little discussion about something and when I finally turned around I had forgotten about those steps. I landed on my ankle with my foot twisted under. I grabbed the railing so that I did not fall. A couple of the waiters rushed over to see if I was okay.

I said I was fine and went back to the table. I knew that it was a really bad twist but I felt confident in calling the Entities in to help with this. I sat at the table quietly for a few minutes. No one really noticed because there was so much conversation! I asked the Entities to come in and heal my foot and ankle. And, you won't believe this (there's that famous line again!)... I had no pain, swelling, or bruising in my ankle!

Another time I was sitting in current in Boulder and an interesting thing happened. Let me give you a little history first... in the late '80s I was in a motor vehicle accident which left me with a herniated disc and whiplash. For two years I was in constant, intense pain. Over the years, with the help of various therapies my back got stronger and my pain dissipated. However, I still continued to receive chiropractic adjustments every couple of months to keep my body feeling at its best.

While sitting in current one time my back started adjusting itself. I wasn't moving at all! Do you know that "pop" you get when a chiropractor adjusts you? I kept hearing those pops... and feeling them! I couldn't believe what was happening and I was concerned that

I was disturbing other people... I could not stop these adjustments! There were about fifty adjustments that night! Since that night about four years ago, my chiropractor always tells me that my back is not out! Previously, my back was never perfectly aligned when I went to see him... and now it always is. I still go about twice a year because I bought a package deal and want to use them up!

When I think about health and healing in the future I imagine it being this way for more and more people. I believe we will more readily become in tune with the spirit world and we will be able to ask the good spirits for the help we need. Indeed, we will have a direct line to the Entities!

Being back in the hustle, bustle of Boulder I would sometimes forget that the good spirits were still with me. At those times I would often ask for a sign. They always give me very clear signs that they are right here with me.... guiding me, supporting me, and helping me every step of the way. One time when I was doubting that the spirits were still here with me I said, "Please let me know that you are here... I cannot feel you with all of the busyness here! It seems so loud here... I cannot hear you speaking to me." I continued on with my day heading into the health food store to get some things I needed. When I came out of the store and placed my bag in the car and I heard a voice clearly say, "Your melotonin is not in the bag!" I knew that wasn't my voice and I found myself taking all the items out one by one. As I placed them on the seat I said to myself, "This is crazy! I can't believe I am doing this... taking all of these items out of the bag!"

When I got to the bottom of the bag there was no melotonin! I went back into the store and asked the cashier if she forgot to put it in the bag. She apologized and said, "Oh, here it is!" to which I replied, "That's okay... a little voice told me it was still in here!" Now, that is the upside of living in Boulder! You can say those kinds of things and you don't get locked up for being crazy!

Since spending time with Medium Joao I have become quite good at distinguishing what is my voice and what is the voice of spirit. It can be a challenging situation in our culture when people hear voices. Sometimes it is because they are in touch with the world of spirit. They can be labeled mentally ill because we do not recognize communication with the spirit world here. And, of course, not all people who hear voices are mediums. Some do, in fact, have psychological pathologies, but, wouldn't it be great if psychologists and psychiatrists understood that both exist?

Dr. Wayne Dyer and his leukemia healing

In the fall of 2011 I went to see Medium Joao at Omega Institute for my fourth consecutive year. It was a delight to see Wayne Dyer at the gathering. I have been a fan of his for a very long time and appreciate his sincerity and his humanness. Dr. Wayne Dyer has been a self-help author and motivational speaker for decades. He initially resisted the idea that his work had to do with spirituality but that has dramatically changed over time. In the 1990s he included components of spirituality in his book *Real Magic* and later discussed higher consciousness in his book *Your Sacred Self.*

During this Omega visit Wayne Dyer got up on stage and shared the story of his leukemia healing with Medium Joao. While working on his book, *Wishes Fulfilled,* Wayne heard about the healings that occur through Medium Joao from a friend of his, Rayna Piskova. Rayna is an M.D. and an eye surgeon in California. Though Wayne had initially agreed to go to Brazil for healing he later changed his mind because he was completely focused on finishing his latest book without interruptions. As Rayna headed to Brazil she asked Wayne if he would be open to a surrogate surgery and Wayne said yes.

Rayna took Wayne's photos directly to Medium Joao and asked if she could serve as a surrogate for Wayne. Medium Joao said that Wayne must start on the blessed herbs first. After filling the prescription, Rayna mailed the herbs to Wayne in Hawaii and he took the herbs as prescribed. After taking the blessed herbs, he took some new photos which he sent to Rayna and when she presented these new photos to Medium Joao he said that now the surgery could be performed.

On April 21, 2011 the surgery was performed on Wayne through his friend and surrogate, Rayna. Wayne had a dose of skepticism and wondered how someone could perform a surgery from 10,000 miles away. Following a surgery the protocol is to be in bed for a minimum of 24 hours. Wayne decided that since he felt good he would go for a walk but about a hundred yards from his home he collapsed on the beach. He started to think that maybe there was something to this and he went to bed where he rested for almost a full week while his daughter took care of him.

Eight days following the surgery it was time for the stitches to be removed. Though Wayne was starting to believe this was real, he states, "I had a modicum of doubt still swirling around in my mind about spirits removing invisible sutures." Despite the doubt, he felt that something divine was going on. He felt like his eye had been scraped and he had been infused with love.

He describes it as though his ego had been washed away and was replaced with an overwhelming divine and peaceful feeling.

During the time his sutures were being removed Wayne had a $17,000 watch with him; a watch that was two weeks old and was guaranteed to never lose a second. This watch lost eighty minutes that day. Two days later the same watch inexplicably lost another eighty minutes. The following day Rayna called him and told him that the clock in her car had also lost eighty minutes. The Entities love to give us signs just in case we still have any doubt! Wayne recognized this as visible proof of some very unexplainable events. Rayna hypothesized that the electromagnetic field of the Entities is much more powerful than the field of the watch. The vibration in Abadiania seems to be faster and higher than anyplace on the planet. Wayne said that what happened to him during those eighty minutes was a divine experience. He felt that he was God and he no longer identified with his body, accomplishments, or anything he has done. His ego had been washed away and divine love filled that void.

Wayne says that since then he sees everything out of new eyes... eyes of love. He experiences himself as pure love and everything he sees is pure love... every person, every tree, everything. He adds that "profound changes have taken place in my body both with a physical sense, and even more empathetically, in a feeling sense."

Twenty days after the suture removal he heard a voice that said, "Do not go for a walk today. You can now do yoga." Wayne, who had practiced "hot yoga," called Bikram yoga, had to give up yoga for over a year because it was too stressful. During that time he says he was sleeping until 10 or 11 in the morning and was getting lethargic. People would say to him, "You don't look so well." Now, he was told that he was healed and that he could go back to doing yoga in a hot room. Today his ability to hold poses in the heat has surpassed what he was able to accomplish before his leukemia diagnosis. Wayne says that after the removal of the sutures everything in his life changed.

Following this healing Wayne continued to feel an overwhelming sense of love that dominated every waking moment. On his 71st birthday he was compelled to share his love and to give to people. He walked the streets passing out fifty dollar bills to street people. Later, back in his room, he just sobbed in gratitude and said that he has never had such a memorable birthday. He continues to give his love, listening, and caring to all people he meets – both people that he knows and people that he does not know. His love continues to overflow.

Wayne Dyer absolutely trusts his experience of what happened with the Entities to the point that he does not need medical evaluations to prove anything to anyone. He has an internal knowing that, without a doubt, he is absolutely one with God. He says that he is no longer simply a loving person but, rather, that he is Love. He adds, "I was transformed with the encounters with John of God, and I rejoice in giving love to everyone and everything I encounter." Every morning now he asks what he can do to make someone else's life better. He is touching people's lives in a way, he says, that he would not have been able to had he not been infused with this love from the Entities. Finally, he says of his mystical experience, "There are many things I do not understand and I like it that way." *

* You may read Wayne Dyer's story in its entirety in his book, *Wishes Fulfilled.*

chapter 7

New Friends, Old Friends, and the Dogs of the Casa

A new reality

As I sit here in a café in Abadiania there is a sudden downpour and the water flows down the street like a river. There is not drainage on this street, yet, it is warm and now the cooler air feels so good. Writing in the cafes here is great and I am enjoying the mochacino and the music in the background! Being near the Casa is like being in another world. It is a world of higher consciousness where the vibration is so high that people can heal to the very core of their being. It is another reality... so very different from the reality that we are typically immersed in. Love, caring, and compassion permeate the air. I feel as though I am living in the world of spirit when I am here in Abadiania... so grateful my journey took me here.

I want my miracle NOW!

With each visit to Medium Joao my symptoms improved and my happiness level increased. I discovered that I was not permanently damaged after all! Rather, a whole new level of compassion for people and for human suffering had been cultivated. At this point I had been to visit Medium Joao six times. With the help of the Entities I had been totally healed of the stalking, insomnia, depression, anxiety and many other things I had asked for... and some things that I had not asked for.

Westerners often come to the Casa and they want their miracles and they want them quickly! I always tell people that although spontaneous healings do occur, they need to know that it could take time and that they will likely see big improvements with each visit. When working on a soul level to clear dis-ease there can be many layers of healing.

Additionally, people must understand that they need to do their part. The Entities have often said that they will do 50% and you have to do the other 50%. This means following the protocols exactly as the good spirits have set them forth. The protocols can include such things as dietary restrictions or abstinence from alcohol and sexual energy for up to forty days. Since we have free will, some people may decide that these things are more important to them than their healing. If someone cannot go forty days without a drink, then his drinking is more important to him than his requests. One needs to be willing to make these simple changes. Then the spirits will know that you are sincere and they will help beyond what you can even imagine.

If an Entity says, "I can heal you," then you can rest assured that it will happen. It may take time. We must remember that the spirits are working on a soul level and not on a superficial level. Living in a society where people often want quick fixes, this is not a path that all will chose. One must be patient and trust if they are to heal in this way.

Ruthann's story

On one of my trips to Abadiania I brought fifteen photos with me of friends requesting healing. It is said that you should do your own healing first and then bring your photos to the Casa. Since I was to be here for a month I created a beautiful altar in my room with Casa crystals, triangles, and my friends' photos.

A long time friend of mine, Robin Goldberg, was here at that time and was staying at the same pousada where I was. Robin is an osteopath and is a doctor whose opinion I respect. One day she looked at my photos and I told her a little about each person. When I showed her my friend, Ruthann from Asheville, I shared Ruthann's story.

Ruthann was born with a heart condition that sometimes caused her heart to race at about 200 beats per minute. Though it did not happen often, when it did happen it could become life threatening if she did not get to a hospital in time. Ruthann was considering a procedure called a heart ablation but she was not totally sure about doing it. Robin said, "NO! Tell her not to do it! That is the CRAZIEST procedure ever... they kill off part of your heart. It's insane!" Whoa... I had never seen her so animated about a Western medical procedure.

I got online and wrote Ruthann but the message disappeared and just as it got lost in cyberspace I received a message from her. She informed me that she finally got an appointment and has decided to go ahead with it. This was a very difficult decision for her and she had to really get her courage up to do it. Knowing this, I did not think the timing was right now for me to send her an email telling her what a horrible procedure it is.

I looked at Robin and said, "Well, if she really isn't supposed to have this procedure, something is going to happen and they are going to give her a call and cancel on her." Those are the words that came out of my mouth but I can assure you that I did not really think that was going to happen.

Ruthann was scheduled for Monday, January 29. On Friday afternoon, January 26, I walked by Medium Joao with her photo to get her herbs. On Saturday morning I received an email from Ruthann that started with, "You WON'T believe this!" I cannot tell you how many times people start with that statement when they talk to me about Medium Joao! Anyway, she proceeded to tell me that she had received a call from the hospital and all of their instrumentation for this procedure mysteriously broke down!

Later when we spoke on the phone we both had a good laugh as we knew exactly what had happened! The spirits were messing around with medical instruments again! Ruthann proceeded to tell me that she knew she was not supposed to do the procedure but she needed a sign. The guy who called to cancel said they had to book out for two months because they did not know what was going on. Ruthann replied, "Oh, that's fine... no problem..." Puzzled, the man told her that everyone else had been upset with him as he made the calls and he thanked her for being so understanding! Needless to say she did not re-schedule!

The dogs of the Casa

The next morning I headed off to Sunday Service at the Casa. It is a beautiful service where people share about their healing experiences, say prayers, and sing a LOT! One Sunday there was even a deeply heart felt marriage proposal. You never know what will happen here but it is always beautiful and sweet.

During this service a woman from New Jersey got up and shared a story. She said that earlier in the day she was at the triangle praying to God for help. Pleading to the Entities for assistance, she was feeling very alone in her troubles. After she prayed she sat down on one of the benches in the assembly hall. Suddenly, she felt a strong thump against her leg. No, it was not an Entity! It was a great big dog!

The dog crawled up on the bench next to her to comfort her. He continued to inch his way up nuzzling his face under her arm and eventually hugging her with both of his paws around her body! She dropped her head down and cried for fifteen minutes as this dog embraced and comforted her.

The dogs of the Casa are amazing creatures. I delight in observing them and marvel at how in tune with the energy they are. So loving, gentle, and sweet, they can steal your heart away. In the year to come I would personally experience just how special these dogs are and how they communicate to us.

Sitting in current, and sitting in current, and sitting in current!

I spend a lot of time sitting in current while in Brazil. Before experiencing current with Medium Joao, sitting had been very difficult for me. Perhaps it was because I had been in that motor vehicle accident a couple of decades ago which caused some bodily damage. Or, it could be because I never let go of my mind as easily as I do when I am near him. Maybe it is a combination of both my body and mind going into a state of deep relaxation where everything is perfect just as it is.

It amazes me that I can sit here for four hours and enjoy it. Though the time flies by for me, I no longer tell the guests on my trips that it feels like forty minutes. On my first trip as a guide two people said lightheartedly to me, "That did NOT feel like forty minutes!" Indeed, everyone has a different experience!

One day in current I was floating through hundreds of crystals and they were going right through me. It was as though I was under water as there was a floating sensation and it was totally silent there. I merged with the crystals and then I floated forward, seeing more crystals of a multitude of colors. I watched with total amazement as we continued to become one and then float on by. "What crystals would be next?!" I wondered with anticipation. It was quite an experience to become one with all of those crystals!

Often I feel bolts of energy shooting through me when I sit in current. My arms or legs jump spontaneously on occasion with the energy. Sometimes it goes through my back and spine with an uncontrollable sudden jolt. Frequently I find myself traveling through time and space while sitting in current. I will be in places that I have not been to before. Recently I was in Viet Nam during current. I have never been there, yet, I was experiencing it as though I was there. Wherever I go, I simply watch and enjoy the journey!

Meeting Silvia and Bill, two surgeons

Medium Joao loves to get M.D.s up on the stage to witness the surgeries... and sometimes to even participate in them. On one of my visits he had a surgeon, Silvia, up on stage. She was holding an instrument tray and there was a man leaning against the wall ready for a physical surgery. Then, after making what looked like a four inch incision in this man's belly, Medium Joao asked Silvia to stitch him up. I didn't realize until I was talking to her later that this was unplanned. Many things here are unplanned!

Silvia looked cool, calm and collected as she methodically stitched him up. Her first thought, she later told me, was "But I don't have any gloves on!" Medium Joao gave her a needle and thread and she took her time to carefully administer five stitches. Meanwhile, Medium Joao slowly wandered around the stage as he waited for Silvia to finish. Normally, he puts in only one or two stitches and he does it in a matter of seconds. He seemed patient as she stitched and he scanned the audience. Suddenly, a woman near me crashed to the floor. It was not as though she passed out but it was a sudden and heavy fall. Medium Joao then said in Portuguese, "She has been operated on. Take her to the infirmary." and someone came with a wheelchair and took her away. Later at the pousada I asked Silvia about her experience. She told me she could not believe the crudeness of the needle and thread and that it was very hard to get the needle through the skin and she kept hoping the thread would not break.

The next week there was a young man at the pousada named Bill. Bill and I had talked briefly but he did not mention that he, also, was a surgeon. The next thing I knew Dr. Bill from Baltimore was up on stage! Later I asked him to comment from a doctor's perspective and he said, "It's a good thing the Lord was there!" His thoughts were the same as Silvia's... "No gloves! Horrible needle! Weak thread! Only two stitches!" With a beaming smile he shook his head delighting in the miraculous nature of things here.

My new friend Janet

I have met many wonderful and fascinating people on my trips to Abadiania. This environment fosters friendship and a strong sense of community. Love, compassion, and deep honesty permeate the conversations. As you sit sharing meals with people you have just met, there is a feeling that you have known each other forever.

On one of my trips I became friends with an actress from the United States. We became quite close as we had two weekends together when we were the only ones in our pousada who spoke English. She shared her life with me doing what I would call a "life review." What a fascinating life she had! I knew as she shared her life that she did not have a lot of time left on earth and this was a completion for her.

This actress, whom I will call Janet, had amazing grace and dignity. With cancer throughout her entire body she was in an extreme amount of pain. Having worked in pain management for many years with biofeedback, I asked her to rank it for me on a scale of one to ten. She was almost always near a ten and she told me that her doctors were not treating the pain.

Yet, she carried herself with elegance and a smile on her face. Only once did she cry and she knew her time was coming.

Janet asked me one time if I would have come here had it not been for the horrible things that happened in my life a few years earlier. I said, "No. Would you have come here if you did not have this cancer?" to which she replied, "No." We pondered upon why it takes such pain in a person's life to be moved to such a place of grace and we both agreed that we were so happy that we had been directed here... whatever it took.

Pain often catalyzes people like nothing else can. It can take people to a whole new level in their lives. Truly this is a place for anyone on a spiritual quest. Yet, somehow it attracts those of us who are ready to open our minds, our hearts and our souls to healing because of the pain we feel. Often it is only when we face crisis that we begin our journey of deep spiritual seeking. We might not have taken this journey under any other circumstances, but, when our health fails us, accidents happen, or trauma occurs, suddenly we become much more open.

Frequently I meet people here and they have totally forgotten what originally got them here. Someone will say to them, "How is your lyme disease?" or "How is your cancer doing?" and people will often respond, "Oh, I've completely forgot about that!" This whole experience is about something so much deeper than what originally got us here. Needless to say, not everyone will be healed on a physical level. Some people come when it is just too late for that. That was the case for my new friend, Janet. She did pass away just a few months after we met. Though our time together was short, I was honored to have met her. Even those who do not receive physical healing tell me that they don't regret their journey because they have come to a place of peace they have never known. I know that Janet is in that place of peace right now.

This book downloads to my surprise and my resistance

On one of my visits to Brazil I had two surgeries by the Entities. As I have said, I love having the surgeries... probably more than most people! My body gets very heavy and it is a visual ride for me as I travel through time and space. I just lie there and watch the show and drift in and out of sleep for the twenty four hours. They are most enjoyable for me!

During my first twenty four hours in bed most of this book downloaded into my consciousness as I re-lived my visits to Medium Joao over the past years. People I have met along the way came in. I had a full review of my journey with Medium Joao. It was amazing and made me very happy as I enjoyed reliving this movie in my mind. Yet, I was quite surprised that I was being told I would write this book. Writing a book is a big project and I never thought I would do another one. The Entities insisted that it be written.

A week later the person on stage at the Casa announced that Dr. Augusto is open to taking anyone who wants a surgery and is willing to follow the protocol. I quickly got in line and off I went for a second surgery. The next twenty four hours in bed were extremely difficult for me and I had what seemed like a "bad trip." It was the complete replay of what happened during the kidnapping and three years of stalking. I couldn't stop it and it just kept coming.

Until this point my surgeries had been, for the most part, beautiful and enjoyable. I wondered why this was happening. The Entities told me a few things loud and clear. First, they said, I had to go through this as part of my healing and that I had to start talking about it. Until this point in time my lips had been sealed about the stalking and all of the social injustice I had endured. The Entities also told me that my story had to be a part of this book that was being channeled. You can likely imagine the resistance I had to what I was hearing. I kept saying, "No, no, no!" to writing the book and they kept saying, "Yes, yes, yes!" It was like I was having a little war with the Entities! It is now obvious who won this little battle!

One of my concerns, of course, was that this man who had stalked me for so long and tore my life apart would read the book and get triggered in some way. I could not even imagine that nightmare starting up again. Even to take any chance seemed crazy to me.

The spirits were totally insistent and would not let up. Finally I said, "If you really want me to do this I need to know that I am protected and I need a very clear sign that this is the case."

The Casa dogs communicate

The next day I was taking a walk past the Casa down a dirt road that I loved to walk at sunset. On the side of the road were two dogs I always enjoyed watching. They were jumping up and down, playfully biting each other, wagging their tails, and obviously having the time of their lives! Though they were really big dogs, they played like little puppies. I paused for a moment to watch as it was a delightful sight.

A short time later I noticed that one of the dogs was in front of me and one was behind me as I walked. Then they moved and one was on each side. They continued to hover around me like that as I walked. A short time later there were four people coming down the road towards me; three men and one woman. I recognized them from the Casa.

To my surprise the large brown dog in front charged at them with the speed of light. We were all just shocked at what this very gentle and loving dog was doing. It was totally uncharacteristic. The four people walking towards me completely froze as there was nothing else they could do. When the dog got about eight inches from one of the guy's legs, it stopped and looked up at him, wagging his tail, as if to say, "Just kidding!" It walked away with a happy bounce in his steps as we were all left completely baffled by this interaction.

As I slept that night I drifted into a place where I was not sure if I was awake or asleep. The Entities are very active in the night working on healing people. The energy is high and people commonly have disturbed sleep here. I was reliving the incident that happened on the road as I had walked earlier that evening. The Entities said to me, "They were protecting you." I still didn't get it until I said, "Oh, they were protecting me?" Finally, it hit me and I said, "Oh! Is that the sign that I am protected?!" to which they responded, "You ARE protected. How much more of a sign do you need?!" Knowing that I could possibly be risking both my life and my sanity, I said, "Just one more sign! I just need one more sign!"

Sometimes people get confused about the difference between dreams and visits from the spirit world at night. Though they both happen while sleeping they are different and easy to distinguish. Typically a dream has a psychological root. It is usually convoluted and needs to be interpreted before we get the message. On the other hand, a visit from a spirit is straightforward and clear. We will get the communication immediately and no interpretation is needed. This was undoubtedly a visit from the good spirits.

The Entities are busy healing people around Abadiania twenty four hours a day and seven days a week. This healing energy extends out of the Casa. It is felt in the pousadas and all around town; especially when we are silent. The good and healing spirits love to visit at night. I think we listen better when we are sleeping!

The next day as I walked through the grounds at the Casa the white dog appeared out of the blue. As I walked towards the bookstore he was there doing a downward dog stretch and with perfect timing he bounced up and looked me straight in the eye as if to say, "We did good, didn't we!?" He was wagging his tail and looking at me as I petted him on the head and said, "Yes, you did good!" That was a non-verbal communication, by the way! I noticed that some people sitting outside the café saw this interaction and the dog's perfect timing. I just thought, "Oh my gosh! Now I am communicating with animals! What could be next for me?!"

Later that day I was again walking through the

grounds at the Casa. As I walked I noticed an attractive man coming towards me and he noticed me. We had a very brief energy exchange. Our eyes connected, we smiled and said "hi" as we passed each other. Then, suddenly, out of the blue, a dog went rushing by me to take this guy down. The man inched his way over to a bench and sat down and froze. This dog was ferociously growling at his calves. The moment I saw the dog go after him I knew what was going on.

I felt bad that I had asked for a second sign and I said to the spirits, "OK! I don't need any more signs! I'll do it!" The dog instantly walked away; calmly as though nothing had happened. That was the moment I agreed to write this book. I absolutely trust that the Entities are overseeing both this book and my welfare. And, I sincerely apologize to the two men who were involved as the spirit world delivered my signs of protection.

Obsessive spirits and other spirits come for healing

The Entities have said that people that come to the Casa bring one, or many, spirits along with them. This spirit might not be an obsessive spirit, although it could be. These spirits align themselves with the person and come to the Casa because they, too, are seeking healing. They are not always malicious spirits. They could be relatives or other people that are connected energetically.

When Spiritists speak of obsession we usually think of a deceased spirit clinging to the spirit of a person incarnate. However, as in my case, the invasive and obsessive spirit was from someone who is still alive. These obsessive spirits can take pleasure in imposing suffering upon their host. This type of obsession is usually linked to revenge and the spirit wants the victim to know he is doing this. They take satisfaction in destroying someone's life.

In my case, Richard's desire to punish and cause suffering arose from the fact that I left as soon as I knew that things were not as they appeared. Richard had intense hatred and feelings of revenge directed towards me for leaving... to the point that he continued obsessing for three years even though we had dated less than four months. Additionally, spirits like this will often attack during the night; which was true in my case. He used his relative freedom during the night to attempt to obsess me, disturbing my sleep greatly, until my first visit to Medium Joao at Omega.

It was a weakness in my own energy field that allowed the obsessive spirit of Richard to be able to move into my field in the first place. Once these weaknesses in my field were healed, this obsessive spirit backed off. There was no place anymore for him to enter my field. In our culture when a woman is being stalked or threatened by a man in some way, the solution is for her to get a restraining order and a gun! As we know from my story, and countless similar stories, this usually does not work. The issue is much deeper... something in the soul level.

The disobsession process can be slow and the longer the obsessor has been with you the slower it will be. For me this process happened very quickly once I found Medium Joao. I will be forever grateful to him and the Entities for helping me with this. As for my part, Spiritists will say that the victim of the obsessor must forgive. The victim must ask forgiveness for the interaction and let the obsessor know that it is time to move on because the relationship is not good for the soul of either person. With the help of Medium Joao and the many good spirits here, I have been able to forgive.

It is sometimes said that healing is finding love and compassion for ourselves... *and* for those who have hurt us. Forgiving the man who stole my life away for so many years was part of my healing. I have come to a place of compassion for him. His pain, hurt, and trauma are very deep and have not been healed. What I can do is ask the Entities to send loving energy to help with his healing if he chooses to accept it. I have asked the Entities to ease his suffering. And, I trust that he is receiving spiritual healing from the good spirits. As for me, I have come to a place of peace in my heart.

Oprah comes to the Casa

Oprah came here to the Casa in the late part of March 2012 to experience Medium Joao first hand and to interview him. March had been a difficult month for Oprah as she had to lay off 30 people from her Oprah Winfrey Network (OWN).

Oprah witnessed Medium Joao perform a visible surgery on a woman whose arm was paralyzed. Joao invited Oprah to come closer to view the surgery. When he made an inch long incision in the woman's breast Oprah thought to herself, "Yes, that is a real knife, and yes, that is real blood dripping down her white pants. How is that happening without anesthesia, without her even flinching?"

As Oprah watched, her fingers got hot and heat filled her arms and chest. Feeling this sensation of heat is quite common when experiencing the powerful energy here. Then Oprah felt like she might explode and she thought, "Is my body bursting? Am I passing out?" In spite of reminding herself to think calm thoughts she was concerned that she might throw up right on camera. Oprah knew she needed to get herself to a chair to steady herself.

She made it to the chair and Heather Cumming, John of God's translator, handed her a bottle of water. Oprah said, "I don't know quite what's happening to me" and she slowly sipped on the water. She felt like she was a bit out of her body and she focused on getting grounded back into her physical body.

Oprah then closed her eyes and focused on on her breathing. Tears of gratitude started to flow as the energy inside of her began to move. Suddenly, she was feeling grateful for *everything* that had happened in her life... not just the things that had gone "right" for her... but also the things that had gone "wrong." Then, an overwhelming sense of peace came over her as she felt a smile inside about all the unexpected roads she had been taken on in the journey of building a network. And, she knew that it was in perfect, divine order that she had been placed here in the presence of Medium Joao where she was given this new and clear perspective.

Oprah left the Casa feeling peace within and the heaviness of needing to let people go from her network had lifted. A wonderful healing occurred for Oprah during her very short visit.

*The article in its entirety may be found at http://www.oprah.com/spirit/Oprahs-Experience-with-John-of-God-Oprah-on-Lifes-Journey.

chapter 8

Sharing These Blessings with Others

Showering all good things

My ability to communicate with the Entities directly grew stronger with each subsequent visit to the Casa. It wasn't anything I was consciously working on but it simply was happening. As I became healed it was a delight to share this healing with others. Finally I was at a place where the healing no longer had to be about me.

One day I ran into a neighbor of mine and he was very distraught. I could feel his pain deeply as he told me that IBM had laid him off. Getting new jobs in the tech field was now hard and he was very concerned about how he would support his family. His wife and two children had stayed up in Minnesota while he came to Boulder to work and he would travel back there to visit.

I decided to ask the Entities for help in my Boulder John of God group, unbeknownst to my neighbor. In Boulder I have a group of people who regularly come to events I lead to share the work of Medium Joao. When I lead current the spirits come in very strong! The first time this happened I was almost knocked over by their entrance! I just did not know what to expect and did not know we would feel them so strongly. I quickly discovered that when I lead current the Entities really make their presence known. Many other spirits come in as well, including spirits of friends and family of the group members. These spirits have also helped in many surprising ways.

After sitting in current I invite people to speak into the circle and request help from the Entities for others. I spoke first requesting financial help and peace for my neighbor. About a week later I saw my neighbor packing up and loading a U-Haul. I had heard he was going to move back to be with his family. I went over to him to say good-bye and wish him well. He was totally beaming as he said to me, "You won't believe what happened! IBM just asked me if I would work from my home in Minnesota! They want me to work remotely! I hope I can get a week or two off to go fishing with my kids first... I haven't had time with them in so long."

This was better than I could have even imagined! Now he was going to be able to be with his family *and* he had his job back! The funny thing is he would always ask me about this "guy in Brazil!" We never got into deep discussion but on some level he had a connection. He would say, "Maybe someday I'll go there with you!"

Time to step up

When all that I had come for had been healed it was clear that it was time for me to share the amazing work of Medium Joao with others. One day I asked the Entity about becoming a guide he responded, "Yes! Absolutely!" The Entity looked at me as if to say, "It's about time! We thought you would never ask!" I think that was Dr. Augusto as he always seems just a little bit impatient with how long it takes me to get things!

There is no way to fully express my gratitude for all that Medium Joao and the Entities have done for me. How do you thank someone for saving your life? How do you thank someone for bringing miracles and giving your life meaning and joy after traveling through the dark night of your soul? My journey with

Medium Joao and the Entities has been life changing. I am honored to give back by sharing this great healing journey with others.

Hearts in unusual places

When this shift occurred and my focus became on helping others, I did my first surrogate surgery for my long time friend Ruthann Hoffman from Asheville. You might remember that she is the woman whose heart ablation was cancelled when all of the instrumentation in Asheville mysteriously broke down the day I gave her photo to Medium Joao. Though she wants to come here, if her heart started racing on this long journey she could be in trouble. We agreed on a date that I would walk by Medium Joao to ask if I could do a surgery for her. He could have answered in one of four ways... no surgery right now, yes and we (the Entities) will do it directly, yes and another medium will do it, or yes and you may be her surrogate. He responded with the latter.

I emailed Ruthann right away to let her know what he had to say and she prepared to do her part. She was to be sitting in meditation, dressed in white, while I went into surgery. Then she needed to follow the twenty-four-hour protocol, the eight-day protocol, and the forty-day protocol.*

The next morning I went into surgery for her not really knowing what to expect since it was my first time being a surrogate. I held her photo over my heart and thought of her. The surgery seemed like it lasted only a few minutes. Again, it seemed subtle; definitely not lightning bolts! But when they said we could open our eyes I realized just how strong the energy had been. In my mind I just heard "wow!" and knew I needed to get to a taxi quickly and get to bed in my pousada.

The taxis are lined up outside the assembly hall and I got into the first one and was back to my pousada within minutes. After I got to my room I had five to ten minutes of emotional release. I cried and felt very vulnerable. Then I started having my usual visual show and eventually drifted off to sleep.

I was awakened a couple of hours later for the blessed soup which was lovingly brought to my room. The soup, blessed by the Entities, is part of the protocol for healing. I did not go back to current in the afternoon but had a quiet day at the pousada instead. Later, I emailed Ruthann to let her know the play by play details of what happened and when. Of course, I was curious to know what she was experiencing on her end.

---

*Appendix 1 in the back of this book explains the protocols that a person needs to follow after a surgery or if they are taking the blessed herbs.

The next day after her twenty-four hours in bed I received the following email from Ruthann about her experience of the surgery...

"At about 7:30 yesterday I felt the weirdest sensation on my Rt. calf--outer aspect...I'd never felt anything like it before--kind of like something was crawling up my leg but on the inside. Then it happened again about 12 hrs. later--it lasted just a few seconds...not a full minute I'd guess. I also experienced the emotional release --early on so it was probably at the same time as you...some crying but not for long...I thought about my mother & wondered what was happening to her when my heart was being formed. At 8:30 I drank some blessed water & went to bed. Mindy (Ruthann's dog) came & got up by me & was sniffing all around me--something unusual for sure. She stayed by my side most of the time. I didn't let her in the room when I was having the surgery, but after I went to bed she was with me.

I asked for a clear sign so I'd know that my heart is "fixed", & I heard the words " you will see hearts in unusual places." Yesterday afternoon I got up & walked to the fireplace to look closely at a print Jimmy (Ruthann's son) had done while in school... it has trees... & there were not leaves--but definitely hearts on the limbs & falling from the tree....I'd say that was definitely hearts in an unusual place!! I hadn't looked at the print up close in a really long time & was not consciously aware of the hearts. But I'll be keeping my eye out for other such signs too of hearts in unusual places.

This has been quite an amazing experience to say the least--I kept your photo with JOG with me thru out the 24 hrs. & when awake felt so connected to you both. Thank you!!!!!! I love you! Ruthann"

The signs of hearts in unusual places continued to come. The very next day Ruthann emailed me saying, "I received the most incredible email from a friend today... it was a series of photos in which people were posed in positions to make them look like flowers....the very first one, had poses that formed hearts... within the flower!" She sent me a copy of the photo and I must say it was quite amazing! Soon after that she looked out her kitchen window and noticed a weed in her back yard with heart shaped leaves.

The following day Ruthann was talking to her sister Kathy, who had a friend visiting. The friend immediately noticed a heart shaped basket and asked Kathy if she could take a photo of it. As it turns out, this visiting friend travels around the world taking photographs of hearts, most often in unusual places!

The theme of "hearts in unusual places" continued on for three days following the surgery. Ruthann told me that she knows beyond a shadow of a doubt that her heart is now healed. One day when Ruthann did not answer her cell phone her daughter got concerned that she might be in the hospital. Actually, she was out paddling a boat! Later Ruthann declared to her daughter, "I am healed! There is no more heart problem!" And, her daughter knew this was the truth.

In gratitude

Since seeking help from the Medium Joao, and the good spirits that work through him, all I asked for was healed. I have saved all my requests to the spirits since my very first visit at Omega. When I look back on these requests and all the miracles that have occurred for me during these years I cannot help but to be eternally grateful and deeply moved. The Entities that come through Medium Joao have literally saved my life. They brought my spirit back and made my life worth living again.

The healing I've had with Medium Joao has gone to the very core of my soul. For thirty five years I have been an active spiritual seeker... meditating, laughing, loving and drinking in life. Though I have done deep and intense work, none has gone to the depths of my soul like the work of the Entities that come through Medium Joao. Being here quenches my thirst and I have come to a place of peace and happiness that I have never known before.

As my journey continues I am forever grateful, humbled, and blessed. Thank you, Medium Joao, for saving my life, giving me a second chance, and showing me that, without a doubt, miracles do exist.

appendix I

*PROTOCOLS**
Set Forth by the Entities

The blessed herbs:

The blessed herbs are powdered passionfruit in gel caps that have the exact vibration in them that your soul needs for it's healing. Most people are totally fine with passionfruit but occasionally a person will have an allergic reaction. This can result in stomach upset or other symptoms. If this happens, contact your guide and he/she will instruct you as to what you should do.

There are four simple things to remember when taking the herbs.

*These are just some of the guidelines and protocols. There is much more to know but this will give you a good, general idea of what to expect with the protocols so that you can make good decisions. If you decide to do this, decide to do it as the Entities suggest!

1. No black pepper, white pepper, or hot peppers; bell peppers are fine.
2. No alcohol
3. No fertilized eggs
4. Take 3/day until the entire bottle is finished.

Protocols following a visible or invisible surgery:

The first 24 hours...

Absolute rest for 24 hours. Take a taxi back to your pousada and get into bed as quickly as you can. Your guide will direct you to the taxi and will take your prescription for the blessed herbs to get that filled for you. Your guide, or someone else, will bring you a bowl of the blessed soup and will bring you meals so that you can stay in bed. These surgeries are powerful and your body needs time to assimilate what happened. Also, your energy field is wide open during this time and you should not expose yourself to other people's energies that may not be helpful to your healing. Stay in bed and do not read or look at a computer. Most people are quite tired after surgery, but, if you are not, just pretend you are sleeping and keep your eyes closed as much as you can.

For the next eight days...

Take it easy and do not do anything strenuous. Do not do any exercise (biking, strenuous walking, yoga, etc.) during this time. Give the Entities some uninterrupted time to work on you. Do not lift anything heavy; if you are flying home have someone else lift your suitcase. Stay out of the sun as much as possible. When walking in the sun, use an umbrella. Give yourself a lot of "alone time" and time for relaxation / reflection. Be sure to leave a note in the prayer basket with information as to where you will be sleeping on the eighth night (and other required information) following your surgery. Your guide will help you with this.

On the seventh night...

The seventh night following your surgery will be a Tuesday if your surgery was on a Wednesday. On that night place a small glass of the blessed water on your bed stand. Before you go to sleep say a prayer asking the Entities to complete your surgery and remove your stitches. Go to bed between 10 and 11 PM and stay in bed until at least 5 AM. Wear white, loose fitting clothes to bed. In the morning say any prayers that you would like to say, thank the Entities for their help, and drink the blessed water.

The following day...

You may go through the revision line so the Entities can see how the surgery went and tell you what is next for you. If you are no longer in Abadiania you may go through the revision line on your next visit.

For 40 days following your surgery...

Do not allow any sexual energy to arise (alone or with others) as this will interfere energetically with the healing. If this is not your first surgery it will only be eight days. Continue to take it easy with physical exercise. Get back into your exercise routine very slowly and gently. Do not receive any body work or energy work for forty days. This includes chiropractic, massage, and any form of energy work. If you have any questions about this, ask your guide. If you are a practitioner you may resume your work on others.

Protocol following an intervention for the eyes:

If you asked for healing of your eyesight it is critical that you abide by the guidelines the Entities laid forth if you want success. Follow the other post-surgery protocols and do not read, do email, look at a computer, watch TV, or write for eight days. I knew someone who did not follow these guidelines and she got extremely sick with diarrhea and vomiting. The Entities are energetically working very hard to help you and you need to do your part.

testimonials

Comments from Casa Group Participants...

"Kelsie did a great job as our guide! We got a lot of information before we came and that helped prepare us. I would recommend her – in fact, I would like to come back with Kelsie on her next trip and bring my mom with me. I highly recommend her."

—Lisa Brone, M.D.

"I CERTAINLY would recommend Kelsie as a guide! She was great about all the preparation... and she picked a wonderful place for us to stay... She is very caring... and she has a GREAT sense of humor... we laughed a LOT!"

—Carol Smith, fellow traveler

"Aside from being gorgeous... (thank you, Ged!) ...and having a vivacious personality – Kelsie really does take care of you. Kelsie has been a great guide for me... she has a lot of levity in herself and expresses that very well... and she's really on top of things!"

—**Ged Thompson,** sit down comic

"You, Kelsie, are a wonderful guide – very organized and compassionate... and you certainly thought through everything in advance. I appreciated the camaraderie we had with you and that you inspired in all of your friends and guests on this trip."

—**Jack Butler,** fellow explorer

Surrogate Surgery Recipient...

"Kelsie was a surrogate for my healing and I am forever grateful! She explained very clearly what would happen in Brazil and what I needed to do during and after the "surgery" as I was in Asheville, NC. Kelsie was so loving and I felt totally connected to her and to John of God and the spirits who work through him. I have no doubt at all that my healing was a complete success!!"

—**Ruthann Hoffman,** Healing Touch Practitioner

Kelsie is a beautiful being of light and love. She shines with compassion for mankind and I am in deep gratitude for her generosity and service. Since I cannot go to Brazil I started taking the herbs and sitting in current that Kelsie leads in Boulder. Miracle's in my life started to happen!! My mothers spirit appeared to me after nearly 40 years of my searching for her. The Entities have healed us both enough to finally connect. This was a very profound healing for me and I am overflowing with Love. Other miracles have occurred and I am ever so grateful for John of God's work... and that Kelsie is sharing his work with us.

—**Kathryn Brooks,** John of God Boulder Group
Participant

The "current" meditations that Kelsie facilitates have been extremely profound, and on many occasions I have felt the spirits of deceased family members and close friends. Kelsie's spiritual blessings and her connection with John of God have affected the depth of my meditation. In one of the meditations a deceased friend came through from the spirit world and told me that she is helping my son who is in need of healing. I was surprised by her entrance and deeply moved. I have a depth of calmness and balance within me since I have made this connection with John of God and I have not even been to Brazil yet!

—**Lynne Faudree,** John of God Boulder Group
Participant

about the author

Kelsie (Kenefick) McKinney has a Master's in Professional Studies (MPS) in Humanistic Psychology and Education from the State University of New York at New Paltz. She was considered to be a pioneer in the educational system which was appreciated by many but not by all. In the early '90s, after teaching high school in the public school systems for twelve years, it became apparent that it was time to leave the educational system. Kelsie returned to school to become Board Certified in Biofeedback (BCIA certified). Then she co-created the Windham Neurological Clinic with a neurologist and neuro-psychologist and went into private practice.

Kelsie taught yoga for about twenty years and people were becoming healed of various disorders in her classes. They reported being healed of TMJ disorders, headaches, and much more. Biofeedback is sometimes called the "yoga of the West" because it scientifically proves what yogis have known for centuries... we can control a lot of what goes on in our bodies. For over three decades Kelsie has studied various meditation techniques, lived in ashrams, and both studied, and led, groups in raising consciousness. She travelled to India several times to further her studies there.

Biofeedback is the perfect career for Kelsie as she is able to bring science and consciousness together. It utilizes her expertise in education as she now teaches people how to consciously take control of the inner workings of their bodies. Kelsie works with people who have the following disorders: chronic pain, headaches, high blood pressure, anxiety, panic attacks, insomnia, and any disorder that is either created by, or exacerbated by, stress. Seeing notable results with their patients, a couple of doctors encouraged Kelsie to put her program into book form. It took Kelsie twelve years to get her first book, *Migraines Be Gone,* out and available to the public.

Migraines Be Gone became nationally recognized and peer reviewed. After putting Kelsie on the cover of their journal, The National Headache Foundation invited Kelsie to be a feature writer for their journal, *HeadLines,* and she started a regular column entitled, *Naturally Headache Free.* Now she was considered to be a pioneer in the field of medicine which seemed to be an easier arena to forge new ideas than in the educational system. Biofeedback continues to hold Kelsie's attention and in 2008 she released her second book, *The Stress Mess,* which is also biofeedback based.

Today Kelsie works with people around the United States leading them through her biofeedback-based programs via phone consultations. She guides them through her program using her CDs, DVD, book and a home biofeedback unit to support their success. She works with migraine patients and people with any condition created by, or made worse by, stress. You can learn more about her work at www.naturallypainfree. com and www.naturallystressfree.com.

Kelsie is a Licensed Professional Counselor (LPC) in Colorado and is a Licensed Mental Health Counselor (LMHC) in New York. One of her joys is to educate people about stress, how it affects their physical and mental health, and, most importantly, what to do about it. In 2006 Kelsie became a Certified Seminar Trainer (CST) and she presents on the topic of stress at conferences and in the workplace.

Though Kelsie feels very blessed to be doing work in the field of biofeedback, it is her greatest honor to be sharing the work of Medium Joao. Kelsie does not know how she could sufficiently express her gratitude to Joao and the Entities – who saved her life and showered her with absolute love – but she is compelled to share his work. Bringing people to the Casa, and to this amazing man who has dedicated his life to easing human suffering, is one way to show her gratitude. Assisting people in moving through this incredible healing journey and seeing them open up and blossom is the best way she knows to give back to Medium Joao and the Entities.